Copyright © 2021 RDW

ISBN: 9798543653791

DEDICATION

Dedicated to the wonderful community of poets I discovered and continue to discover on Instagram; a worldwide community of diversity, that is constantly growing, evolving, and thriving. You are the lighthouses that bring my ship to shore. You are part of my daily life, and I treasure you daily.

And to all aspiring poets and writers everywhere; I hope this book, and ongoing project, fills you up and inspires you to new heights. I hope it helps you to believe and remember that you are, indeed, a poet.

Yours always,

Ryan Daniel Warner

INTRO

The poetry included in this *'I AM A POET'* anthology is the hard work of 108 poets from around the globe; many who have never had work published before. This book serves as an outlet and opening for their talent. The work was submitted to me for my *'I AM A POET'* Instagram project. My aim being to record many of the poems that were submitted – here in this anthology, and also via a consecutive spoken word project, which can be found on my website – www.rdw.world

This anthology has two overriding purposes –

1) To encourage poets like myself and the poets included herein, to believe and remember that they are, indeed, poets and should use the term often and without shame.

2) To showcase the diversity that exists among poets, and the wide-ranging, ever-changing reasons that we use poetry to express ourselves, make statements, and attempt to understand others, the world, and ourselves. And to bring these different people and reasons together.

There was a huge number of pieces submitted for this project, and only so many I could fit within this book. The pieces included have been selected, because, above all else, they tell stories and relay messages exceptionally well, through their flow and voice, enabling us to connect with the hearts and minds of the poets, and in doing so, with parts of ourselves. We observe how the poets see themselves – through their words, and then we either resonate/empathize or learn new things, thereby educating ourselves in the process.

As with many of my publications, this book may be a little rough around the edges in some ways. Hell, so am I. And so are you, whenever you truthfully look in a mirror. It's what makes us who we are. A few of these poems may have the odd grammatical error, but they are all authentic messages, which we need in this day in age. Above all else, the poetry contained within reminds us to examine ourselves. Who knows? Maybe you're a poet too.

I know I am.

Truthfully, a poet is a creature that tortures itself with a stick called a pen

RDW

FOREWORD
by @DUANETOOPS

My morning begins with a search for words, and, perhaps, the words begin their day with a search for me. Some days we find each other like star crossed lovers brought together by the serendipity of persistence and strong coffee. Some days we are a missed connection. There is only an infinitesimal window within the infinite expanse of time that we can hope to meet. When cast in such a light, the task seems almost insurmountable, if not outright impossible...and yet here we are, together again...

In the life of a poet there are frequent and recurring moments in which the inexplicable force of a thought or an idea storms the gates of our minds and takes tyrannical control over the near entirety of our mental faculties. Like some backwater outpost overtaken and under occupation, we are at the mercy of something beyond ourselves, something powerful and all-pervasive.

There are moments when the work ceases to be our own, and instead we become owned by the work.

To be a poet is to be hunted, hounded, and haunted. To be a poet is to know what it means to be possessed. It is to no longer be in possession of one's own thoughts, but to be possessed by them, to be possessed by something beyond them, and perhaps to be possessed by something beneath them. To be a poet is to yield oneself completely to the unrelenting control of something that is equal parts demonic and divine.

Chuck Palahniuk writes that *"something foreign is always living itself through you. Your whole life is the vehicle for something to come to earth."*

To be a poet is to be a haunted house; to be filled with otherworldly apparitions of the unknowable.

Every lyric is a conjuring; every line an invocation, every word scribbled across paper is both a summons and an exorcism. Every poem is an apocalypse, an uncovering, an unveiling, a revelation; an in-breaking, an excavation, and an arrival.

Poetry creates a breach, a disruption. Poetry creates space; a space for awareness and observation, a space to see and listen, a space for silence to creep into our speech, a space in which the quiet can, itself, begin to speak. Poetry is an invitation to meditate upon the experience of mystery and the mystery of experience.

The task of the poet is to make the mysteriousness of experience palpably vivid in a way that does not resolve the mystery but, instead reveals the mystery as more profoundly mysterious than we realized.

Poets teach us about experience. They teach us about our own experience. They teach us about the way we experience what we experience.

With great care and reverent luminosity, poets teach us to more fully experience our experience. They do this not by teaching us how to put our experience into poetry, nor by teaching us how to experience a poem, but by showing us that poetry is always-already present in experience, itself.

Poetry is the experience of everything. And thus, every experience is an experience of poetry.

We are full of secrets, and poetry is the fossil record of the human condition, maybe even the fossil record of the human soul. Buried beneath the compacted layers of sediment is the history of human longing, the music of our millennia of tragedies and triumphs, the rapturous soliloquy of our radiant splendor, the joy, grief, sorrow, lament, despair, our excitement, exhilaration, and our exuberance.

Each poem is an act of faith; a faith that some minute piece of the manifold mystery will become material for a moment. A faith that some small substance of the things hoped for will become manifest, albeit in an ephemeral way. A faith that we will uncover the evidence of things unseen, the evidence of the possible, and that the possibility will claim meaning.

Duane Toops

a.e.t.f.xo ·

I am an artist
I am a creator
I am a lover
& not a hater
I am refined
But also obscene
I'd rather be real
Than shiny & clean
I am a good person
I am a bad bitch
Yes. I can be both
& I'm also a Witch
I am eccentric
I am very loud
I am never too shy
to show I am proud
I am pansexual
& not afraid to show it
But most importantly
I am a poet

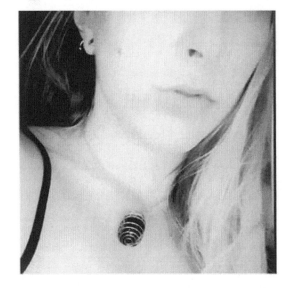

secretwriter1427 ·

I am...

~*SecretWriter1427*

I am simply a skin-suit, a
decorated bag of bones;
I am a palace of flesh, blood,
and memory that my heart
will always call home.

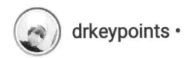 drkeypoints •

I am a poet.
With an overflowing ardor of love and self discovery
My mind is a vessel of concealed battles and beauty
Marked with triumphs and losses
Spilled in a chronicle called life.

I am but a poet.
A soul with a finite days of living and trying
With unending hope to peace and serenity
Under the spell of trials and tribulations
Caught up with a pen and her thoughts
A written history locked in an asylum called life.

I am a poet.
A thinker scrawled every bit of thought she could hardly stuttered
A wishful dreamer with a sense of gratitude to everything that matters
A believer redeemed and found under an immense love of Christ
I am a poet - existing in every line of both fortune and faith
I am a poet - a humble promise
Continuosly writing her story in a book called life.

DR.KEYPOINTS

 k.m.writes_ •

⋮

I am a poet.
Poetry flows
through my veins,
thus I bleed ink.
I don't shed tears,
I embody every
e m o t i o n
through poesy,
I bring words to life
and let them breathe.

Oh darling,
you won't die on me
for I can make you
i m m o r t a l
through my piece.

~K.M.

@k.m.writes_

 **lostincloudysky** •

⋮

I am trapped
somewhere between Neverland
and never being as young as I was yesterday.

Dizzy from being thrust forward,
full throttle,
eyes sinking into my sockets,
flesh gradually decaying at a cellular level,
mind bombarded by the incomprehensible
volume
of information,
emotions a haphazard tangled mess.
Externally calm,
internally ablaze.
Overloaded and overwhelmed.
A fine line away from diving
headfirst-

All the while gazing across
to the perfectly balanced horizon,
the ombre sky of pink meeting the turquoise
sea,
in beautiful harmony,
tranquil and at peace.
The salty air tickling my face
as I inhale deeply the magic which surrounds
me,
and exhale all that torments,
finding myself again the way I always do.
amongst the noise and the chaos.

And though anchors tied to my feet
attempt to drag me down,
I remain afloat.

You see,
it is madness out there,
but in amongst it all,
I find the beauty.
Can you?

glass half full | lostincloudysky

noraravenspeaks ·

Queen of the macabre

-Nora Raven

I am a poet

They say I am Queen of the Macabre

But I bring light out of the darkness, baby

Watch me do magic, abracadabra

They say it isn't easy loving a poet

My therapist told me there are untold stories

Buried underneath those memories

But I bring structure to those disordered lines, baby

I am made of black magic, do re mi fa sol la ti

beboldtoya

I

am

proud   of

ME

for

standing   up

to

ME

ihave_writes •

I am learning...
Learning to love myself in the ways
    I begged to be loved from others
Learning to hold space for the parts
    of my body I once let fall to the floor
I am more of the person I was told I wasn't
    than I am of the person I was raised to be
I am sorry for being the last person to
    realize that I should accept you for me
I am aware of how deep your cuts run
    for it was me who dug them into your ski
I am desperate to heal on the outside
    so that you may grow from deep within
I am nurturing my once dead flesh
And with each and every morning breath
    I breathe life into what was
I am a fighter who will hold on tighter
    in the moments I feel like giving up on us
I am you
You are me
And I've fallen in love with who I've gotten to
Embraced in the hands that felt your pain
I am sorry I ever let you go

—Candice Leigh

 **jmarie_voe**

I Am A Poet

I
Am
A
Poet
That expresses herself in a colorful way
Swift and sharp like the game of archery
Striking targets revealing what's hidden in the heart
Typical colors can rhyme without issues
The one I am requires you to really use your mental
Breaking codes that hold delicate petals
Carefully choosing what creates the perfect unity
Blended with attitude that pushes any ego to the floor
But also displays a love that accepts what others say
leave at the door
Bright yellow lifting spirits
Sprinkles of laughter to hit souls differently
Stallion strong different paths of topics at the crossroads
Covered in red courage and passion
Creates an imperfect harmony from the collision
Your happiness is my yellow happiness
I'm uplifting
Uploading things to make you smile
Feeling warm inside

J Marie

17

 **jmarie_voe**

I Am A Poetic Maniac

Your pain is my pain
Loyalty is deep within my roots
I can't swim
But I'll choose to drown before I let anything bad happen
to you
Exposing myself so a person can relate
Shedding habits that broke me
Replaced them with yellow moments that have been
sunshiny
Friendly red fire pushing you to your greatest potential
Especially when it felt like it was
Unreasonable
Unreachable
I'll let you know anything is achievable
Understand I'm here
I've been labeled
It's my duty to turn the messed up tables
Into a dining area where you take your seat
I Am A unique definition of poetry
Bold and outstanding
Thrills from my rollercoaster that'll create something
foreign
Ask me what color best describes me I'm quick to say the
color orange
I
Am
A
Poetic
Maniac
Coming in for the kill
With my ink filled gun
Ready for the massive attack

J Marie

 **patriciahelenwriter** ⋮

I AM

I am someone I've just met.
I am someone I used to know.
I am someone in discovery
and the process has been slow.
I am a wee child who was broken.
I am a woman inching toward light
who'd buried deep dark memories
pretending everything was alright.
I am someone seeking a reconnection.
I am someone who's seen god's energy.
I am a perfectionist in all that I do.
I am driven to be the best I can be.
I am a wife...a 'Baba' and a mother.
I am a teacher and a lover of books.
I am a poet who finds poetic expression
absolutely everywhere I look.
I am an introverted people lover.
I need time alone to recharge.
I am someone who loves the night.
I am at one with the moon and stars.
I am probably very ordinary.
I am likely like many I have met.
I am determined to move forward
for my journey is not over yet.

 **nicolejadepoetry**   ⋮

I am more than I thought
but less than I wish
I'll describe it in a way
much simpler than this.
See, we desire what we've not
then abandon all we've got
Single mother pushing harder
to replace a missing father
Widowed man fulfilling a list
his late wife sadly missed
Broken poet breaks again
to relive better times with her pen.

No matter the rough
through the complicated and tough
you must remember
that you
are already enough.

NicoleJadePoetry

lerosewriter •

I am a fragment of a universe
A page in a book that is steeped in blood
Scarred, black memories that I cannot grip hard
enough to extricate the lies
I am lungs split open by too much empathy,
emotion crisscrossing my throat like thorned stems
And I cannot breathe

I am a writer
But only when the memory of his hands is
gripping my skin
Like majestic teeth, wolf blood soaked;
Gripping tightly around my neck
I am the girl, late home, knee deep in a hidden
river whittling words in the confessional of my
spine
I am all the words spat into my viscera
Words I twisted into a crown that adorns the ruin
of my wanton skeleton
I am the sermons of youth that forced the devil to
secrete his flesh in me
I am the unwoken
I am nothing

Luna Rose

 emm_kay0 ·

⋮

I am

A little sprinkle of stardust
Shimmering in the soul of verses
Shining in all the unsaid words that
you hold close to your heart
In all the words that have found
utterance in all the voices far and
apart
A miniscule wave in the sea of life
lost during the high tide
I am all the oceans in all the
universes and multiverses
Storms and waves I ride
Smaller than an atom
Bigger than the sea
The paradox is me.
©emm_kay

poetry_ordeal_solitude_solace_ •   ⋮

I am a crumpled book
No matter how straight a word may look
It's alphabets will always seem unfathomable

I am a torn page
Even if you try to align its halves and read the lines
It'll always remain meaningless

I am a leaking pen
No matter how hard I try to jot my heart down
It'll always get stained and smudged

I am a ruined colour
No matter how perfectly I try to paint
The colour will never reflect it's true shade

I am a distorted poem
Even if you wanted you could never read
me with a rhythm
I am a ruined poet!

I am a poet!

But I am still a book
It'll just need one flip at a time to see
through my opacity

And I am still a page
That'll need a pure soul's endeavour,
to recite my poems

Also, I still am a pen
One that is still breathing and that can
still write, even if it's hard

I am still a colour
It doesn't need to be exact if I can paint the
blankness, doesn't matter the shade

I am still and forever a poetry
In which, rhythms lie within its vulnerable words,
if you'd know better
I may be ruined, but I'm still a proud poet!

©HIDDEN DEMOISELLE

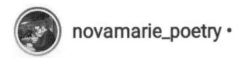 novamarie_poetry ·   ⋮

I Am A Poet

My fingers know the
weight of the pen
because it holds so
much more than just ink.
My skin knows the
texture of paper.
Knows the bite of
paper cuts and the
sharp crinkled edges
of crumpled pieces
thrown across the room.

novamarie_poetry   6/30/2021

24

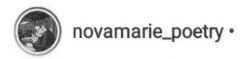

novamarie_poetry •

⋮

I Am A Poet

My back knows the pain
of sitting in one place
for hours trying to get
every word just right.
My feet know the tapping
of anxiety and frustration
when things sound better
in my head than they
ever could on paper.

novamarie_poetry   6/30/2021

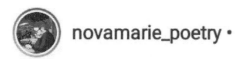

novamarie_poetry ⋅

⋮

I Am A Poet

My chest tightens
at the thought of
writing my last poem,
knowing that there's
a good chance that
even I won't know
which one that will be.
But for now my pulse
dances through my body
because my heart beats
in iambic pentameter.
I'll probably die
holding a pen.

novamarie_poetry   6/30/2021

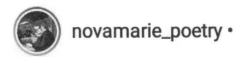 novamarie_poetry ·   ⋮

I Am A Poet

You can see it in
the midnight shadows
that rest under my eyes
from writing well into
the night and early morning.
See the smudge of
smeared ink on the side
of my hand like a bruise.
With my pen to paper,
I punch out poetry.

novamarie_poetry   6/30/2021

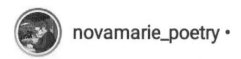

novamarie_poetry •

⋮

I Am A Poet

My bones know
the dull ache of
unwritten pieces
hidden in the marrow.
Sometimes poetry feels
like breaking bones.
My blood holds secrets
and I will bleed
to discover them.
Even if that means
bleeding out.
Because...

I Am A Poet.
It's just what we do.

novamarie_poetry   6/30/2021

 the_realm_jumper ·   ⋮

I am a poet, filled with incomprehensible passion...
fueled by madness,
A wonderer... my mind is curious... it goes down the
rabbit hole like Alice...
I am love...the embodiment of light, and the universes
vastness...
And death, embracing a deep connection with my
darkness.
I am a black sheep, sent off to slaughter, for fear of the
power I possess,
a soul on fire...an enforcer, engulfed with justice and
purpose...
I am a rain conjurer who dances life back in when the
storm surpasses.
She is me, I am her... a lover , a fighter, a survivor, a
mother...ME... a monster... a poetess.
🖤 Ruby Jane

k.m.writes_ •

⋮

I am a warrior,
a fighter, a survivor,
I've been living
in a hole of darkness,
war in a battlefield here
are dreadful and endless.
I've fought with tears
and blood, saving myself.
If you reckon to wreck me
with wrongful judgement,
you can no longer hurt me
even just a single threat...
For hell, is now my friend.

~K.M.

@k.m.writes_

 jeam.precious •

⋮

I am a poet.

I feel and breathe poems
in the midst of the unknown devotion,
singing softly to myself in the shadows
while painting stars in the sky
with words dancing in a mesmerising
lullaby.

I am a work of art,
an expression of my heart,
I write with love of light from the sea
a sound of heart in thunder melody,
where I am my own riddle and mystery.

Kiss my haunted lips and meet my soul.

-precieux

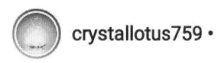

crystallotus759 ·

⋮

I AM A POET

I am a poet, I ponder, I wander, in a moment I live centuries.
I stroll in the allay of mind , labyrinth of memories.
I stand long where two roads bifurcate.
I see the green woods turning into yellow woods ,makes me late
My destination is very far now thorns prick in every stride.
yet i see colours of growth in the darkness of monochromatic nights
 I am ephemeral but my poems and stories shall survive.
In all the hearts those were once broken learnt to strive.
My words for hearts are the fallen rain drops on the barren land .
Promising for better tomorrow by blossoming hopeful songs in the present .

crystallotus

 **realmpoetry** ·

I am a poet
My imagination is around the corner
I live and die inside the paper
Through my words, I become a savior

I am a poet
I can reach my dreams in the skyscraper
In poetry, I became an interpreter
Through my phrases, I become braver

I am a poet
My verses are much louder
I can see myself much prouder
My thoughts become much charmer

I am a poet
Even though I got a wrong grammar
Still, I am not a spammer
My world of ideas is like an armour

about_a_heart •

I am an indigo child
who's guided by the moon,
In a world of conspiracy
I'm seeking my life's truth.
My head lives in the clouds,
only place I can't be used,
anonymously recall on paper,
when my mind began to skew.
I am a paradox to some,
a fun-loving contradiction.
Who's soul was rendered numb
writing stops my heart from bleeding.

About_a_Heart

Indigo Child

 **autumnalfyre** • ⋮

I Am

I am an art museum, a concert hall
A guessing game, a masquerade ball
An accent you can't quite place
A name you don't remember but a familiar face
The lingering scent of bonfire night
A shadow cast by candlelight
A somber event's comic relief
A flawed, fragmented masterpiece
The liner notes and the cover art
Of the album you have yet to start
An outdated atlas in the library
The forgotten corner of the cemetery
The thoughts that come when the night is still
Make of me what you will
I am a riddle and a mystery
I don't know yet what I want to be

@autumnalfyre

lexanne.poems •

I am a soul drifting
searching for deep connections
I feel a lot and deeply
No one truly understands what I feel
I can only unleash all my feelings into poetry
I am a soul that doesn't belong to this era
I am an old soul
I find solace in writing
I can only go back in time through oldies
I am a lonely soul

@lexanne.poems

lexanne.poems · ⋮

我是漂泊的灵魂
寻找深层联系
我多愁善感
没有人真正理解我的感受
我只能把所有的感情都释放成诗
我是不属于这个时代的灵魂
我是一个老灵魂
我在写作中找到慰藉
我只能通过老歌回到过去
我是一个孤独的灵魂

- 瑶琴

lerosewriter •

⋮

I am a seance
Within
Place your hands on my vastness
Fingertip to fingertip
Spread wide
Invoking the spirits that roam these ruins
My realm is widening
Hawthorn laced thighs
Your carcass drawing out the need in me
A need to be seen
Woken
Touched
A need to show you I live; I feel
Even if only until
You force this beast to be exorcised
Only until
You offer your lips in resuscitation
For the pulsing ghost
Tied within the bondage of my soul

Luna Rose

 **poetrybyaiden** •

I am an actor who acted to distract me from myself,
I reacted with other actors and transformed into something else.
That reaction gained traction and became a compulsion,
An obsession to consume souls to their utter repulsion.

I pretend to every end that I'm a victim of my addiction,
But the truth is I'm petrified of my valediction.
What I want can't be prescribed on prescription
And it doesn't exist purely in the realm of fiction.

So if I look a little tired of being sick,
And pulling tricks for your attention.
You'd do well to understand beyond your pretension,
That I am what I am without any comprehension,
And I'll do whatever I need to fulfil my intention.

@poetrybyaiden

kindle.downs •

⋮

I am always forging a new identity
Daughter sister mother
Life
A circus ball
It keeps me on my toes
Healer preacher sinner
Smelted in life's fire
Bent and twisted
Shaped to fit
Victim perpetrator woke
I trust in the steady anvil
The study hammer
I dance to the blacksmiths tune
Grieving crying bleeding

— Linda Downs

glittersofthought •

⋮

I'm a poet out of metaphors
my inkpot is dried and the quill is lost
the thoughts amalgamatimg with words seeking paper

I'm a poet out of metaphors
i want to sugarcoat my scars, by describing
the passive pain into something beautiful

I'm a poet out of metaphors
and this midnight silence urging me to write the melancholic poems,
emerging from the wild heart

I'm a poet out of metaphors
caffeinated, not so sophisticated
putting fragile heart and chaotic mind in a weighing scale to balance my poem

I'm a poet out of metaphors
juggling with emotions
struggling with phrases
tangled in expressions

I'm poet out of metaphors
i have papercuts on my wrists that bleeds stardust in night

@glittersofthought

sticksandstonespoet •
Melbourne, Victoria, Australia

I AM A POET A WRITER OF WORDS
I DARE NOT SAY
BUT DEEPLY FELT ALL THE SAME
A PAINTER ARMED WITH A PALLET
OF COLOURFUL VERBS
BOLDLY I DECLARE
LET THIS HEART TRUTH BE HEARD
NOT ONLY BLEED ONTO PAPER
EXPRESS THE FEELINGS
OF HEART AND HEAD
FOR WHAT USE IS A HEART
IF I CANNOT TELL YOU
IF I ALWAYS CHOKE
ON THIS STAGE OF LOVE

FOR PITY'S SAKE LET IT BE SAID

YET COME CURTAIN CALL
ANOTHER MUTE PERFORMANCE
OHHH WHAT IS LEFT TO SAY NOW
POETRY IS DEAD

@sticksandstonespoet
©dmccarthy

Quotes Creator

 r5k.poetry •

I am more than a man, I am a work of art,

I am more than a poet, I am an expression of the heart,

I am more than just words, I am exposing my soul,

I am less than perfect, I am sometimes an asshole,

But no matter what, I am always honest and true,

I am not me unless I am with you.

RK.

 dwainswords •

"I am hope
wrapped in soft linen,
I am vibranium steel
used as armour
shielding my emotions"

_____

Dwain Brown

 dwainswords •

⋮

"I am my mother's child
giving birth to possibilities,
nine months of struggle
and hard labour
lead me towards
who I am today"

Dwain Brown

 dwainswords •

"I am peace and war
fighting for balance,
I am the locksmith
opening doors, for the next
generation
moving into a home
filled with tranquility"

Dwain Brown

lexanne.poems •

                   ⋮

I am a poet
I pour out all my suppressed feelings
and weave them into poetry
I have shed tears
so I understand broken hearts
I have been to the dark abyss
so I understand the hopelessness
I have got out of the sea of despair
so I know there is hope
Poetry made me alive again
It did so for many others
Poetry is alive

@lexanne.poems

loveletters_ransomnotes •
Melbourne, Victoria, Australia

```
        i am b and Iamb
    Is this a riddle or poetry?
    Does 'b' stand for bleet?
    as in baby sheep? Oh sheet!
 'ear pleasing' rhythm: iambic feet
   lines from Shakespeare I repeat
   listening for accent short or long
   I know my heart prefers whale song
   (a sound called 'boing')
   (oh boy! Onomatopoeia joy!)

        i am a poet breaking down
    suffocating in syl/la/bles
       drowning in de/scrip/tion
          wallowing in words
            no wonder poets frown!
    if 'stasis is the basis'
       then poetry is dead
          I live playful language
            flowing fluid in my head
              I'm proper
              I m proper
              always human
            sometimes a poet
```

covid_killed_my_career •

I am a green leaf.
I am a juicy leek.

Truth is a green leaf.
Absorbing all that shines,
soaking in nourishing light,
rejecting the unneeded type.
Is the leaf truly green,
or is that the only thing
the leaf can't accept
and therefore reflects?
The green is all we see,
and enough people agree,
so that is what we believe.

Truth is what we seek.
Truth is a juicy leek;
circular and layered,
spectacular yet wayward.
Is the leek occluded,
self-protectant and weak,
unable to accept critique,
or encapsulated in mystique?
The shelter is all we see,
and enough people agree,
so what is it that you believe?

adanakaz_poetry •

⋮

I AM A POET

I AM A POET
Am I really?
Is it because
our words and rhymes
give us the wings to fly
To touch the sky
And be as limitless
and free
as can be?
Is this Poetry?
Our destiny?
Is it words in tune with
soulful frequency
harmonising with spirit
in this synchronicity
giving our lives
a deeper meaning
adding value
and sparking
an enlightened being?
I am a poet
Am I really?
Whatever you believe
Its not down to you
So, I am a poet
This is the very essence
of me!

Written by Adana
AdanaKaz_Poetry

kindle.downs •   ⋮

I am a fairy queen
Tinkerbell of promises
My whole life dedicated
To somebody else's wishes
I grow weary with the weight
The corrupt unbalanced scale
I promised
I'd be a good girl
Be respectful and kind
Speak when spoken too
Swallowed those cruel lessons
Your secrets
A hot cauldron held close to my chest
Scarring more than skin deep
So when I promised to obey
I wasn't ready to be loved
But a promise is a promise
A holy communion with fate
Take this body
Take this blood
Devour if you must
What little I have left to give

– Linda Downs   YourQuote.in

thedarksideofthephoenix •

I AM SHRINKING WHILE I AM GROWING
I AM BOTH COMING & I AM GOING.
I AM STILL HURTING, YET I THINK I AM HEALING,
I TRY TO BLOCK IT OUT, BUT I AM STILL FEELING.
I AM THE FIRE THAT LIVES UNDER YOUR SKIN,
THOUGH I AM AS COLD AS ICE WITHIN.
I AM LOST, BUT FINDING MY WAY,
I AM FULL OF DARKNESS, IN THE LIGHT OF DAY.
I AM IN A HURRY, BUT GOING NOWHERE FAST,
I WANT THIS TO END & I WANT IT TO LAST.
I AM NOT A GAMBLER, BUT THE DIE HAS BEEN CAST,
LOOKING TO THE FUTURE, WITH MY HEART IN THE PAST.
I AM ALONE, BUT SURROUNDED BY HIM,
I AM ALWAYS LOSING, EVEN WHEN IT'S A WIN.
I AM A WARRIOR, BUT I FEEL SO WEAK,
I AM HIDING FROM THE THINGS THAT I SEEK.
I AM MOSTLY UNKNOWN, BUT I WANT TO BE HEARD.
I AM A POET, BLEEDING MY THOUGHTS THROUGH MY WORDS...

poetry_on_edge_of_life ·
Aalborg, Denmark

I AM...

I AM TODAY
AS EVEN BEFORE
EVER WILL BE
TODAY I AM
DARK

I USED TO BE
LOVE AT MY CORE
PEACE INSIDE
AGAIN I'LL SEE
LIGHT

I AM TODAY
SAME AS BEFORE
SAME AS WILL BE
TODAY I AM
ME

@POETRY ON EDGE OF LIFE

 amylouiseliddy •

⋮

I am a poet.
Words found me before I noticed - light, heavy,
non sensical, scribbled in ring bound notebooks,
where daydreams from school windows and feelings
from old music became letters balanced on lines.
Unfinished, belonging.

A memory from a swing, ponytail and ripped jeans,
set away from playground laughter,
aching with a certain kind of melancholy
for nothing you could really put your finger on,
except the cheap biro or the Parker cartridge pen held
between thumb and forefinger, that lived in the drawer,
patiently waiting for the story.

 **amylouiseliddy** ⋮

I am from homemade A5 books, roughly folded
and sellotaped from A4 paper, carried in a bag everywhere,
with felt tips and crayons.
Pieces of paper collected, old letters from granny's house.
Your rubbish, my treasure.

A short girl with dimples, age 5 verse speaking 'My sister Laura'
by Spike Milligan, every word, intonation
and facial expression engrained in me decades later.
Crisp white shirt, blue striped tie, first prize certificate
framed in the lounge, above the worn beige sofa
forever disassembled into a den, lived on and jumped on
by 3 siblings facing a brown TV set with 4 channels.
Books and stories, stories and books.
Dad always told them best, the Irish delivery, unrivalled.

 amylouiseliddy •

⋮

I am a poet.
The observer of subplots within small groups of people,
tip-toeing along the edges of inclusion,
a pair of nervous butterflies in the stomach grew
into wide winged birds, deep thinking, restless,
imaginative, free, yet often lost in the vast expanse
of worldly possibility and the physical limits
of being in one place at any one time.
War poetry in year 11 did little to ignite a fire in me,
who really knows where they are going at 16,
how sweet and fitting it is to be *open minded, curious.*

amylouiseliddy •

I step within and step out of all that is seen
and unseen by the eye - brown, blue or green average.
Strangers pass me in the street and I wonder
about their story behind a smile or a hello -
what makes them wake up at 3.15 in the morning -
an empty stomach is an open wound in a silence
that is deafening - you all know what I mean.
I wear your shoes and walk around in them,
empathy connects and depletes for the writer,
the unconscious narrator.

I take solace in the words I find when the present
becomes the past with the voices that fade
when the memories stay.
And from this I create, create, create.
I am a poet, at peace with a pen.
And I am from all these things -
all the shoes I have yet to wear
and all the words I have yet to write.

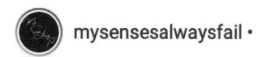

mysensesalwaysfail •

I AM... I'M NOT SURE.
AM I AN ECHO?
AN ECHO OF TIME FRACTURING
IN EVERY NEW RIPPLE?
I COULD BE ANYTHING I WANT,
ANYTHING I PUT MY MIND TO,
BUT MY MIND IS BURIED BEHIND
EVERY GREY CLOUD MADE BY YOU.
DESPITE MY INFLUENCE
THE DEAD WILL REMAIN DEAD,
WANTS AND DESIRES FOREVER LOST
FLOAT ON THE BACKS OF EVERY WORD UNSAID.
MY SOMETHING TO LIVE BY
WILL BE OTHERS TO DIE BY.
I KNOW WHAT I AM OR AT LEAST WHAT I'LL BECOME.
I'LL BE A FIRST DANCE TO A FAVOURITE SONG,
I'LL BE SOMEONE'S FIRST GOODBYE.

I AM MOMENTS GONE WRONG.

—MySensesAlwaysFail—

 ryandanielwarner

'*I AM THE RABBIT*'

I am my own imperfect, inconsistent self;

/

the body that bleeds, the knife that strikes;

/

the poverty that haunts the wealth,

/

the resistant rabbit, who, when kicking up the dirt,

/

digs his heels in,
stands his ground,
and knows his worth,

/

until it hurts

/

that's who I am;

/

that's what I'm like

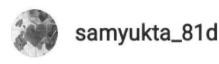 samyukta_81d

~~I am confused.~~ *I am figuring it out.*

~~I am a coward.~~ *I am braver than I think.*

~~I am gullible.~~ *I put a lot of faith in humanity,*
sometimes too much.

~~I am naïve.~~ *I am still learning.*

~Asta

thediffidentspeaker ·

I am nothing but a fleeting moment
The hand of a clock running in full circle
I am of life and love and confusion
Sometimes, I am nothing but paper
Floating and then soaked in water
Until I am dissolved and indecipherable

I am an unfinished chapter, a story never written
I am a leaf floating and then falling
Touching dust as if that was the ending
I am who I am
A moment passing in time and eventually forgotten
I am nothing but the beginning of endings

I am a drop of ink and then a piece of paper
And then whatever it is that I can use
Just to define and point out that I am abstruse
I am a flower that blossoms and then withers
A subject of life that is already dead inside

I am who I am, said the philosopher
Then again, after a few years of existence
I ask myself, "Who am I?"
I've never been close to the answer
For I am defined by a series of words
Coming and going, until eventually
For countless of times, I'll just lose my meaning

@thediffidentspeaker

 petren33 ·

I am me,
There's no one else I can be,
I finally see that now,
I used to want to be anyone but myself,
Shelving all of my feelings and my own personality,
Pretending to be someone else,
Anyone else but myself,
Because I just wanted to be liked,
To be accepted,
To not be rejected by anyone,
But in doing so I was rejecting myself,
Putting the real me on a shelf,
I am me,
Not anyone else
And I never can be,
I finally see that now
Because I am me,
The only person I can be,
The only way I can truly be myself is by being me,
I am me
Because that's the only person I can be. @petren33

62

 **iamnickke** •
Thika

Am 96 already
I lived so well
It seemed a fantasy
Long rides across Tennessee
Blue vodka plus Hennessey
Age mates burning with jealousy
A middle finger for celibacy
Sovereign powers to enforce intimacy
And unspoken words to protect the legacy

iamnicke

saint_noah_poetry ⋮

I Am Me

I Am......the howling winds of destiny, vividly Subdued yet gently destructive.

I Am......the tepid gusts of breath, enhanced by life's mysteries.

I Am.....the blessings within a silver lining of the clouds, Beseeching the demons

..Of Every Mother Fucker That's,
........hard done by,
..........down and out,
.........broken and lonely.

I Am......written in the stars.

 saint_noah_poetry

⋮

I Am.....the dusty memories that glide across the fields of home sweet home.

.....I Am WILD!!!
......I Am FIERCE!!!!

I Am......the Snowfall after-life, tiptoeing along the distant melody of my dreams, crying sweet lullabies as i cling on to the Days of yore.

I Am......the Teasing of death, Spreading like hells fire until the Ashy remnants of crushed hope are left to fertilise the Sands of time.

I Am.....the Flourishing lovers, Dancing in the rain yet dry from the cover of perfect intimacy.

I Am.....the Gift of love, as echoes pass through Falling shadows, reaching softly towards amours promise.

 saint_noah_poetry

⋮

I Am......liquid Blossoms, that bloom in wave shaped whispers, Crumbling into the seas.

I Am.......the Bluest moonlight, shining secrets amongst the stars before collapsing into a wondrous ocean of Myself.

I Am....Collapsing into a wonder that is me.

I Am....Collapsing into me.

.............I Am Me

©saint_noah_poetry

 jaimeboey •

I am a Poet

@jaimeboey

I am a Poet, who will fly freely in solace

Grieve the touch and miss the embrace

Cherished clues for carnal Casanova

One more day has gone by

Locked my heart away

from people passing by

Life's mundanity in humanity

Cliché existence aimless blues

In compromising poetic thoughts

And agonizing a wandering mind

O' curse of consciousness

For in a sad closed world,

what could I find?

For a fool's gold?

Rusting flames in my heart burns

Sombre scent in smile and scar

Like Sunset's fate of glorious sheen

Make way to a humble descent

A quiet wish, whispering hush

Over brewing tea's vapour

For someday somehow

A thin rope reveals

To be out of this

spiraling tunnel

One fine day,

somehow.

My soulful heart synthesize as I learn amalgamate when I gather harmonize to be heard for I am a Poet @jaimeboey

 theknifethatwrites •

Soldier of Fortune

I am a figment of my own imagination,
Stuck between yesterday and tomorrow,
A whisper on the wind, unsure and
untrue,
Carelessly strewn across fields of
fortune,
For the past to wonder and the future to
construe.

I am a phantom of my past,
Fighting a sentinel guarding me against
myself...
Forever vigilant;
Lest the catacombs spring to life
And I become the man I used to be,
One more time.

Dev.

poeticifi

I am a force of brown clay, breathing.
An illiterate striving to communicate in the world's
language. I am constantly caught
expressing myself in my own
dialect.I am an art comprised of countless stamps.
A plethora of many scars. A story which has only
begun. A library of several tales. I am a map.
A guideline to liberation. The foundation of a new
generation.A dictionary of every positive word.
I am one great graffiti.A tip of an enormous iceberg.
An encyclopedia of answers.A candle burning
bright,
yet my wax is not melting!

I am by @ Poeticifi

 elliemorfou •

I AM A POET

I am a late bloomer.
Like Alexander Fleming before penicillin
or Stan Lee long before Fantastic Four,
or Julia Child without a cookbook
and J.K. Rowling without a publisher.
I'm Alan Rickman before Die Hard
or Winston Churchill before PM.
I'm now blooming.
And through this all
I've been a soul
trapped in the wrong life by my mind
and fighting back with all I've got,
some paper and a pen
and my true love for words.

@ELLIEMORFOU

lucidlotuspoetry ⋅

⋮

I am a Poet

I am the invisible wind
unseen but not unfelt

I am desert and oasis
stripped to essentials
and ripe with offerings

Shining and reflective
I am the Sun and the Moon

I am a deep body
of mostly water
that drowns itself

But I am also the light
above the dune

lucidlotuspoetry

 **j.h8.6** ·

I am atop these city streets, night skies dressed with silhouettes, dancing on rooftops, my jaw dropped, the rain-swayed-across moonlit pirouettes. Our feet made music to irregular heart beats, awestruck were many sea breeze breathed, thick as thieves we waltzed through autumn leaves, right down to sunkissed city streets. These moments set our hearts on fire, your eyes drowned me in a sea of dark chocolate dreams. Horizons burst with technicolour beams, our serene candy-cotton-neverland-dream. We lay beneath a sea of stars, crowned with halos, weaving dreams from sacred streams. Her voice became the orchestra to my heart. Pretty was this miss-of course, foolish did she make my heart sing-yes. Birds sang quietly warm with low beckoning tone as in confession, whispering sweet hymns-serenely perfectly orchestrating my heartstrings with magnetic-kinetic-energy, filling my lungs with ecstasy.

Written by J.h

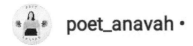 poet_anavah •

⋮

1/2

I am not the name I bear for I have many.
A different name in school, one at home,
A different one you cry out in bed,
While you are grunting between my legs.
I am not my body for it changes.
I am a pound heavier than yesterday.
I don't always measure, nor need to.
Every day my body goes through changes,
Of a God given cycle that makes me bleed.
I am not in pain now but I will be.
I am not my brain, not all the time.
Being clever is hard work.
I prefer to let go, give up control.
...
I am looking for a dominant, not all the time.
Sometimes I don't want someone to answer to,
Because I don't need to. I am my own person

——

SENS_UAL_POETRY

 **poet_anavah** •   ⋮

2/2

I am me, a mixture of all that I can be.
And yet I am still Concrete. Not fluid.
But at times I like to flow.
Flow with time and places, people and faces.
I am Ana, Anavah, Annie, Sometimes NB.
You know my sensual side, flowing poetry.
On my knees I like to be,
In front of you? Not all the time.
I am tears and blood and throbbing flesh.
I am will and mettle and aloofness.
I believe, I question, I strengthen my beliefs.
I doubt, I fall, but not a the time.
I am me, essentially, all the time.

———

SENS_UAL_POETRY

words_by_amey ⋅   ⋮

I Am

I am like a moving picture.

The paper shall remain,

as the bones of me.

But the image, morphs and evolves.

       Transforming.

For all lives many different stages.

Adapting and resilient.

Marked by time.

Experience.

That shall not define me, but remind me.

I am allowed to make such movements,

in how I tend to perceive

Stepping out of my familiar to create a feeling new.

Freedom I am granted to shed the skins of doubt.

Permission I am offered to let my flowing be.

I am a colourfully constant state of change.

Every breathe can motivate the quality of the next.

I am fully alive within my growth.

loveletters_ransomnotes •
Melbourne, Victoria, Australia

I am the trees, the birds, the bees
I am the waves, the sky, the breeze
I am the moon, the stars, the sun
I am journeys begun and coming undone
I am the universe and love's argonaut
I am what I am and what I am not
I am the poetry of perpetual feeling
I am a body with boundaries
in unbounded being
I am a poet

 **adam_s_champion** ·

I am the sum of all my scar tissue
Years of southern soul abuse
Baking humid summers
Where the AC doesn't work
An oil painting caked with layers
Of pain and toxic dirt
Government assist programs
For school lunches, and knock off brands
Poverty and pain my childhood friends
A ouroboros of insanity that eats itself
And starts again, again, again
I am the letters I still write her
Petrol words her eyes a lighter
A pyromaniac until my dying day
I lost my mind in New York City
Where fingers dug and monsters raped me
It made me something wrong,
I'm not quite right
I am frozen core and burning anger
A reflection in the mirror stranger
Sunken bruised fruit eyes and restless nights
I am a poet who takes the home grown hell
And tries to make it right

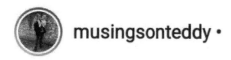 **musingsonteddy** ·

I AM

I am a ship
with broken sails
running aground on rocks
I am a racing car
(your favourite)
veering off course
trying to reach the finish
I am a horse
saddlebags overflowing
with your precious things
I am a pillow
a safe haven
for your soft curls
I am a star
in the darkness
guiding you to safety
I am a circus performer
juggling motherhood
and everything else
I am a mountain to climb
but you
you will move mountains

~ Izzy Thomas

 **poisoned_quill_writing**

I am a woman.

But that is not all that I am.
I am a daughter, a sister, a friend.
A student, a writer, a full-time worker with time still to volunteer

I am bereaved.

There are days when the world seems black with no sight of the light
Yet I still smile
Watching films with others when we're miles apart, quizzes with epic losses and
wins, reading the same book for the hundredth time, with a tear in my mind

I am tired.

Still, I'm the kind of person that pretends they're in Harry Potter when visiting
Durham.
Need a new book or a film? I've got a long list of ones I'll readily recommend
I've been in a street race with someone who's name is long forgotten around the
streets of Lincolnshire

I am in my thirties.

But I still sleep with Ted the Teddy in my bed each and every night
I'll sleep in unicorn bedding, rock my tigger tattoo, eat Cocopops for every meal of
day with a cocktail at night and meanwhile,
I'll watch the Simpsons on repeat as a way to unwind

poisoned_quill_writing

I am beautiful.

With chipped varnish and silver threads through faded hair
Whether I'm lounging in pyjamas or dressed up to the nines
Smiling and laughing with faded eyes

I am fool.

Who wears my heart on my sleeve, will trust people are what they say
I will give more than just a second chance as we continue in the everlasting dance of
trust and deception
And I do trust, implicitly, until given a reason not to

I am forgiving.

But you're yet to make your actual apology to me and not just a pretence in a video
to the world where you say 'I care.'
I watched and I listened and I read between the lines
So until your apology is more than just a publicity stunt - I will forgive myself for
falling for your bullshit and your lies

I am not difficult.

But I **am** opinionated and I will stand for what I believe in each and every day
I will apologise when I'm in the wrong, and I will apologise when you're wrong in the
wrong, but I will make it clear that it was your misconception
My voice may be loud but it needs to be to be heard above the systematic bullying
and abuse so that I can make it through

poisoned_quill_writing

I am not silent.

Still, you try to speak for me, speaking of what you believe to my experiences without
actually asking for my views
Perpetuating the belief that women do not have a voice, that we need someone to do
the speaking for us and somehow believing that even though I should be celebrated
for being a woman -
Apparently, I cannot speak for myself

I am scared.

Not of walking alone
But of how the world is polarising to them and us with no middle ground
Hatred, suspicion and violence round every corner being aimed at all instead of just
pointing at the one to blame

I am not my mental health

But people don't want to see that and instead of talking about how it is for me they
just believe all mental health is how they see portrayed in the news
I'm told that I use tattoos as a form of self-harm when in fact, one covers the scars,
others used as a way of self-expression and others - because I can
Excluded from plans as assumptions are made of how I am, but I wouldn't be
excluded for my physical health so don't use my mental as your excuse to try and put
me on a shelf

 poisoned_quill_writing

I am a goddess.

I am the maiden, mother and crone
Bathed in light from the sun and from the moon I am crowned
So that my past, present and future I can reclaim

I am not just a woman.
I am so much more.
I am me.

© Rowanne S Carberry 12.04.2021

 jullzwolf_poetry •

⋮

I am nobody!

To the majority who would not understand,

I am who I am because most of you can not see

The bittersweet truth of my identity...

Therefore, I proudly be...

Just another nobody...

@JullzWolf_Poetry

muse_and_metaphor ·

i am William Shakespeare
in his literary prime;
i am the 'Star Crossed Lovers'
he kissed with poisoned ink -
i am Da Vinci decoded
with a 'Mona Lisa Smile' -
i am Mozart at the peddle
(de)composing in silk -
i am Marie Antoinette
ascending mediocrity -
i am 'The Real Musketeers'
abstracting aristocracy -
i am Vincent Van Gogh;
brushstrokes of savant insanity -
i am the (f)ear that was 'left'
behind an 'Avant-Garde' tragedy -
i am Jung and Sigmund
in a 'Freudian Slip' -
i am Princess Pocahontas
going down before the ship -
i am Einstein and Hawking
playing theoretical chess -
i am Goddess Aphrodite
in various states of undress -
i am Michelangelo
in the throes of revolution;
i am the 'Renaissance Revival'
sculpting life with absolution -
i am Dante's Divine Inferno,
penning purgatory paradise -
i am 'The Theory Of Everything'
and your universal vice -
i am the Devils Doting Daughter
with a healthy 'God Complex' -
i am the Mistress to your Master
i'll leave all of your demons perplexed.

pj_writes

I am
speaking to you
Look at me
not through me
Can you actually
See 'Me'
I Am.
Yes, I Am.
I had no original voice
No say on who
I would be
No say on how
I would look
I did not set out
to be this way
My Creator
decided to mold me
and make me into this—
'A Vision of Beauty!'
Imagine when I was
just an embryo
No visible form
No model to mimic
No palette
Just a thought

pj_writes

All infancy stages
Didn't know how
I would be revealed
Sure, I had matter
Sure, I had genetic infusion
Transformation
Fleshed
Now.. finished I am
as it was
He who pumped
blood in my veins.
He who blew
life into me.
I became colorized
hued, pigmented
melanated, vibrant
Exclusively unique
Unveiling
a thing of beauty
Turning heads
Double-takes
A topic of discussion
Here I Stand!
I Am.
©pjpayne

 **writerpoetkim** •

I am a Poet
It seems like such
A small statement,
But it has taken me years,
Countless tries,
Exploration a-plenty,
To come to that truth.
How these stanzas -
Groups of words strung like pearls from my mind -
Bring me such joy,
And soothe the ache within.
It's the ache all artists know...
The burning desire to create,
Silencing the cacophony drumming
In our hearts, minds, and souls.
I deepened my understanding of self,
I deepened my connection with others,
I became a whole human being
After I set pen to paper
And unleashed the creativity
Swirling around inside of me;
A tornado of passion-filled words.
How four little words,
Four little letters,
Bring me such joy:
I am a Poet.

@writerpoetkim

josefinlequeen •
Poetry

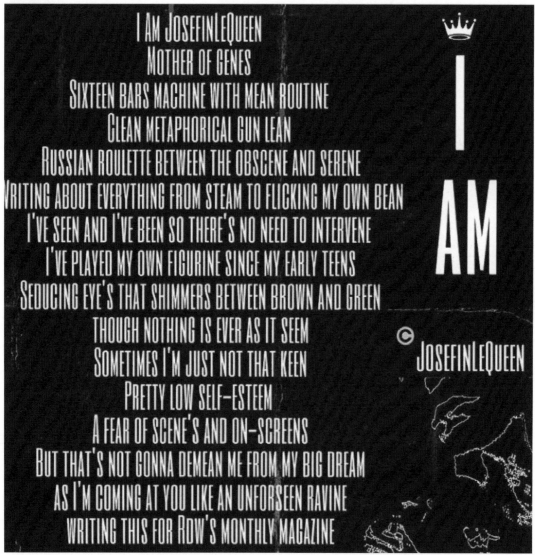

I Am JosefinLeQueen
Mother of genes
Sixteen bars machine with mean routine
Clean metaphorical gun lean
Russian roulette between the obscene and serene
Writing about everything from steam to flicking my own bean
I've seen and I've been so there's no need to intervene
I've played my own figurine since my early teens
Seducing eye's that shimmers between brown and green
Though nothing is ever as it seem
Sometimes I'm just not that keen
Pretty low self-esteem
A fear of scene's and on-screens
But that's not gonna demean me from my big dream
as I'm coming at you like an unforseen ravine
writing this for Rdw's monthly magazine

I AM
JOSEFINLEQUEEN

dr.inkwright •

⋮

"I Am"

I am...concern for humankind
A divine vessel like many, except not blind to my spiritual roots
I am proof that what was supposed to be produced by the environment, can be rerouted to break
the noose
I am star-level focus amidst the mediocrity
The comprehension of a need to dispel hypocrisy I...
Am not worthy of the Creator's love
Yet like Him I wish to show it to everyone still above ground
I...am...tired
//
I'm wired for global impact but temporarily challenged in the space I am in
I am fruit-bearing dreams living with two battle worn feet
Fighting not to give in to rising sins that constantly seek attention
I am my ancestor's answer to greatness, though the journey appears long and tedious
I will defeat this apparent wait and watch God break every chain
I am ready
I am...
calm
I am proud of what I have become
a faithful & persistent
Son of the Creator
Much more will be revealed later
I assure you

@dr.inkwright
(6/11/2021)

penned.piper

⋮

I am an unknown,
 but not quite a mystery
A story untold,
 with deep rooted history
An enigma in contrast
 to honest vulnerability
Just trying to be seen...
 To be someone worth mentioning

My life's been just a shadow,
 yet I am a form
A great shape in the sunlight;
 Golden and warm
Silhouettes and reflections
 never seem to make sense
I don't know myself well
  in the present tense
And all that I am
 seems to contradict
who I thought I was

so I've thrown out the script
And all I can say now

Is that I am becoming
And all I can do is
 keep running and running
and running and running,
 to the sunlight I'm coming
to know my warm side
 as I've known my shadows
to feel the light spread
 until nothing else matters
to learn myself well
 and lean in to mystery
to hear myself whisper
 of foreshadowed histories
to hold tight to my love
 of honest vulnerability

To see and be seen;
That is something worth
mentioning

Trying to know the
 unknowable is rough
But ever becoming myself is enough

Ever becoming myself is enough

-Piper

debbie_o_bottled_up_feelings ·

I am that flower
On the side of the road
That someone has plucked
Because they thought it pretty

They all pass by that same road
And see me
But then they play
That game with me

She loves me
She loves me not
And every petal they pluck
I feel profoundly
As I have loved them all

debbie o bottled up feelings

 joyshribose

I AM A POET

I am a poet
Certainly not the best, yet
Through the prism of poetry
Rediscovering the felicity,
A blessed wife and mother apart
Turbulent ocean of emotions engulf my
heart,
In my world of words, weaving a reverie...
A world free from the shackles of every
Apocalypse, malaise and poverty;
Though I am the favourite child of destiny.

-JOYSHRI BOSE.

picture_me_a_poet ·
Het Balkon in de Zon

I am a poet

I am a poet
It is what I want
Maybe even
What I need to be

June 11, 2021

Steve Hetem
@picture_me_a_poet

picture_me_a_poet •
Het Balkon in de Zon

⋮

I am a poet

3/4

This world is filled with creatives
Painters, sculptors, comedians
Performers, photographers
And many more are creative
In their own unique manner

I write poetry for fun
For the play-on-words
For the drama & laughs
To tell forth my story
To process my emotions

Tell me your tale
Give me your worries or strife
I will twist, turn & transform
Your words & stories
Into prosaic verses

Steve Hetem
@picture_me_a_poet

June 11, 2021

picture_me_a_poet •
Het Balkon in de Zon

I am a poet

I am a poet
It is what I need
If not, I ask myself:
What else would I be?

Steve Hetem
@picture_me_a_poet

June 11, 2021

poetrybyaiden •

I am wired to be insane.
I cry when I'm angry,
Laugh when I'm in pain.
I am repelled by love,
But a magnet for hate.
I hide myself away to compensate.
I am bonded with the dark,
I run away from any light.
I disagree for disagreeings' sake,
Then cower from the fight.
I rely far too much on too few,
Despite wanting to do everything myself.
I fall into depression when I fail,
Then become paranoid about my health.
People look at me a little strange.
Marriage, kids and the nine to five?
To me it seems a bit deranged,
A responsibility suicide.
I analyse myself a lot
But it's no fucking good.
When you're someone different everyday,
It's like an eternal childhood.
I often wonder about the point of it all.
Everything's hard and there's never enough time.
Constantly seeking further extremes,
To feel anything at all and remain in my prime.
In the end what I fear are two things:
Failure and death, before I grow my wings.

@poetrybyaiden

a_place_for_my_words •

I am a whispering enigma
I am a wandering soul
a sprite lost amidst the willows
a woman searching for herself
I am the writer of my thoughts
I am the wind moving in my mind
a woman of little importance
a keeper of dreams
I am a poet

@a_place_for_my_words

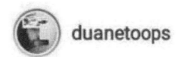 duanetoops

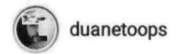 duanetoops

duanetoops Chuck Palahniuk says that "The writer isn't afraid to tell an awful truth. The writer might not be smarter than us but the writer is braver and more honest." My truth, my awful truth, and nothing but the awful truth is that I have a propensity, or, perhaps, a proclivity for being a fuck-up. Throughout my life I have failed more than I have ever succeeded and I can only hope that my honest admission of my awfulnesss makes me brave.

Life often feels like a vast and ever-widening collection of moments that I cannot change; a collection of profound instances in which I should have known better, an amassed assortment of words and deeds that I have either done or said that can never be taken back, undone, or unsaid. And yet, when I am at my most uncertain and my most unsure, I am proud of my children, I am proud to be their father, and I am proud to be a father.

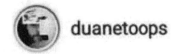 duanetoops

Karen Rinaldo says that "on the other side of frustration and discouragement [there] is tenacity and hope". I know that this is true because I know that on the other side of every devastating obstacle and lonely heartbreak my kids are there. Together they are my North star, ever guiding me towards home. They are constellations bursting through the black of the bleakest night with the fierce tenaciousness of hope.

I know that there is some light left in this world because my kids are in it. I know that there was once some light in me because I still see it in them.

I may not know who, or what I am, but I know that I am their father, and that is more than enough...

secret_words_of_hart • ⋮

I am the invisible human being
Who's rarely heard and equally unseen
For twenty odd years I have not existed
Now my whole world has totally shifted
My life plummeted into a heap
I found myself writing extremely deep
For if I did nothing I'd be extremely sad
I think if anything, I would go completely mad
Poetry has saved me from the depths of despair
It's odd really as I didn't care
I'd lost everything that I had ever known
A car crash, relationships
and a house I called home

ellen_writes_poems •   ⋮

1990
after @goldlacedink

I am all of the family that came before me
I am a mother - heart full and joy unbound, yet exhausted with
worry and bone weary
I am a wife but my name is mine; from my family, my lineage

I am invested in friendship - the precious people I treasure and
relationships I nurture year after year.
I am heart swells when I think back to who we were at 5, or 13, or
18 and how we have grown together;
a bond deepening each decade

I am nostalgia, wrapped up in memories of bygone sepia tinted
summers

@ellen_writes_poems

 **ellen_writes_poems** •

I am feminism and fire
I am books: as many books as I can cram into my brain and heart
I am writing, processing everything I feel in an iPhone notes app

I am brought to tears and roused into passion by Mitchell, Joplin,
Dylan, Morissette, Winehouse, Spektor, Harvey.
I am dancing to Lizzo, hair tossing feeling good as hell

I am tears, often; raw emotions worn on my sleeve ready to be
exposed at any time
I am drunk, sometimes. Wild with beer, prosecco, dancing,
laughter and on the best days? Tequila!
I am rejecting diet culture, unapologetically eating

I am lust, my husband lighting fires in my belly.
I am partnership, a team as we navigate family life and
domesticity, our friendship the foundation of us

@ellen_writes_poems

ellen_writes_poems •

I am achingly lucky, arms and heart full of little people who were once housed in my body
I am not a perfect parent but I keep growing, keep learning, keep correcting

I am indebted to my mum and dad, the greatest of role models and my dearest friends
I am the youngest of four, two sisters and a brother - my treasured kin; the tightest of bonds and most joyous laughter of all.

I am wrinkled, smile lines prominent after years of laughter and late nights; these lines are a privilege I try not to bemoan
I am 31 and I cannot wait to see what growing older brings.

I am changing and evolving. Ask me again next year.

@ellen_writes_poems

debbie_o_bottled_up_feelings · ⋮

I AM
STRAIGHT OUT OF FUCKS.
I AM
TIRED OF THIS LIFE.
I AM
TIRED OF THE STRUGGLE
AND ALL THE HOOPS.
I DON'T WANT TO JUMP ANYMORE.
I DON'T WANT TO PLAY.
GAME OVER.

debbie o bottled up feelings

poeticbeyond3544 ·

I am
A poet addicted to
Pornographic flesh
and orgasmic breaths
That women make
Wearing naked flesh
I am the same as a
Drug addict instead of
Popping Molly's Rx
I pop Molly's in the flesh
a fiend for ass and breasts
I am a living mess

sticksandstonespoet •
Melbourne, Victoria, Australia

I am the storm
before the calm
disenchanted by heaven
I am inclement weather
constantly
raining on my own parade
I always do everything
backwards
spinning on my axis
a defiant mercury
in retrograde

©DeeMac
@sticks&stonespoet

Quotes Creator

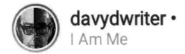

davydwriter •
I Am Me

⋮

I am

I am January – an anthology of backstreet pubs and lost poetry
I am February – writing stanzas on the inside of lavatory doors
I am March – pondering how snow falls on the Underground
I am April – a surprise verse illuminating a stubborn page
I am May – having a tantrum over old northern business
I am June – that man racing camels up and down sand dunes
I am July – old metal rolling on a road to nowhere
I am August – a red fox etched upon a pavement
I am September – slugs of warm gravy swimming in cold custard
I am October – one lit window in a row of sleeping houses
I am November – coal dust and mascara making eyes glitter
I am December – grandad's ancient map curling at the corners

I am

DavyD

lismcdermott •

I am dragon, though no fire do I expel,
but words and songs in various hues.
Within my soul I dance with joy,
memories of my life, I employ
to fuel my imagination;
My love of people is the foundation
for my beliefs,supporting others
as though sisters and brothers;
I am empahty-full, crying far too easily,
when happy or sad – just as equally;
My super-hero force is to empower,
help others grow and bloom like flowers.
Born a singleton, happy in my own skin,
thankful my soulmate's passions to mine are akin.
I am grateful to have lived to this age,
still with plenty of empty space on the page
for my continuing words and adventures,
an unfinished composition to be explored,
expressions to be left as my life's record.

© Lis McDermott 2021

n.matthews.poetry •

I am the people pleaser,
Person watcher,
The sarcastic comments that make you laugh
collector,
I am never sure how I should be,
So I tentatively tread through my days,
Picking up traits that I hope you might like,
I am an anxiety masker,
Society fitter-inner,
I will bend and mould myself trying to fit,
Even though I'm never sure if I ever master it,
Sometimes I laugh after the punchline,
Always hoping you'll laugh at mine,
Avoiding the sting in my head from eye contact,
Makes me think maybe you see right through me,
And all my underlying mannerisms,
I am autism,
And I am everywhere,
You just don't know because we get so good at
going under your radar.

N.Matthews

 **purplebirdcollective** ·

                                         ⋮

<u>A six-word story</u>

I am
but a weeping pen.

@purple bird collective

 a_c_lawless •

I AM

I AM a writer, a record keeper for history,
 inspired and influenced by life's goings on.
I AM a soliloquy, a living, breathing monologue,
 with conversational remarks and witty retorts.
I AM a work in progress, an ever-changing novel,
 each chapter, an alternate ending.
I AM a student, a lifelong learner,
 passionate to peel back layers of knowledge.
I AM a wildlife warrior, a soldier for Earth,
 an advocate for the continuance of this planet.
I AM a spiritual being, an open-minded vessel,
 accepting of all love great and small.
I AM a dreamer, wide-eyed visionary,
 with goals and aspirations beyond what I could see.
I AM nervous, moody, an introvert sometimes,
 ambitious, curious, poetic with rhymes,
 a Capricorn, lived and worn, headstrong since I was born.

I AM...

I AM many things.

secret_words_of_hart •

I am a little damaged now
Which is quite a shame
For my love was huge and my loyalty the same

I focus on my poems
They seem to help me heal
I'm just lucky Instagram has people that can feel

@secret_words_of_hart

save_dbychrist ·

⋮

I am the poetry—
written in my very entity.
The paper shaken glory,
Vexed in all earth's worry.

I am the prose and the lyric,
The rhythm of my own being.
Suffering composed my melody,
Tears assembled my narrative.

I am the testimony.
The words and the longing.
The spaces in between,
The phrases that lingers still.

I am the exclamation,
The excitement in all its error.
The shout and its bouts,
The emotions that has no route.

I am the stanza and the line,
The never ending sigh;
The curves that sometimes rhyme,
But often left behind.

I am the comma,
The pause in every trauma.
The silence in every part,
The period in which i jot.

I am the question mark,
The hardest whys I ever asked.
Written in ink divine,
Stains of pen marred my hands.

I am the preface and the text,
The bibliography and the contents,
The pages and the cover,
The end i long to hover.

YISKĀH

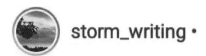

storm_writing •

I am a cargo ship,
large and unyielding,
stuck at sea,
searching every ocean
for a place to call home.

There have been many captains,
men who barked orders,
serving none but themselves.
And unlike Smith of the Titanic
they will not go down with their ship.

Once handsome, pristine,
the maiden voyage with smart navy paint;
now blistered and worn, salt eaten edges.
Iron and water and air collide,
rusting from the outside in.

1/3

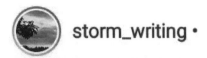 storm_writing •

2/3

At every port,
I am loaded with more containers,
quay cranes
stack sharp edged
burdens upon my breast.

I sigh beneath their
heavy load,
heart nestled and hidden,
a safe room cabin,
far, far below the surface.

Hurricanes in the night,
rolling waves that
crash over the deck,
pitching and surging,
thrown by the storm.

2/3

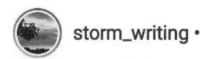 storm_writing •   ⋮

3/3

When I can no longer bear what
I must carry,
shipping crates break open,
plastic debris slipping
into dark waters.

On the winds rage,
hardened hull
creaking with the pain,
yet, miraculously, I remain
afloat when the morning comes.

I long to dock
in sun filled horizons,
and rest awhile, without others'
expectations bearing down upon me.
But still I sail on.

3/3

 **purplebirdcollective** •

I am,
but a weeping pen.
I cried myself to sleep again.
Pondering if my poetic words are impactful enough.
Wondering if my painted art is colorful enough.
Asking if my pleading heart gives out love enough.

I often ask myself too many questions,
fading themselves into the night
and only to be greeted by them again in the morning light.

Are my inked words fragrantly pleasant
to touch you across the other side?
Asked the writer.

Is my art vivid enough
to imagine yourself in my painting sky?
Asked the artist

Is my heart plenty enough
to embrace its beats for both of us?
Asked the dreamer.

@purple bird collective

1/2

 **purplebirdcollective** •

Yes, I cried myself to sleep again.
My teardrops are a testament that I am to be,
they are droplets that water the vine of pain and bliss,
they kiss my face to reminisce of the memento yesterdays
to remind me of my inner worth rising and
believing in my self-ink being again.

Ultimately, God knows my bruises and numbness best.
Even when I want to fight His transcending test.

He says that I am,
more than an imperfect weeping pen.

I have been commissioned pathways
to supply love, light, art, and words
to meet you there with my ever-flowing waterfall.

Even if my rhythmic sobs need to fall
to give my soulful purpose out
the only way I know how
is to love myself abundantly first
to give you all that I Am, after all.

@purple bird collective
2/2

petren33 ·

I am a poet,
I haven't always known it
Or wanted to show it,
I used to keep my work hidden away,
Initially from myself
And then just from the world,
But these words whirled around my head
everyday,
I couldn't let them stay there
So I pieced the words together,
Tethered them down
To stop myself from drowning in them,
That's when I started to feel free
Because it was a way to help let my
feelings be,
To free me from all of my thoughts,
But it still wasn't enough
Because I was still keeping my work
hidden,
Forbidden from the world
Meaning my words were still trapped,
Not completely strapped down,
They were still fighting to get free,
The only way to truly let them be was to
set them even more free,
To share my pieces with the world,
That's when I finally set myself free
Because when I let the world see my
poetry
Something inside me unlocked,
I was so shocked

Because finally something I did
wasn't mocked,
I didn't want to block out the world,
Instead I wanted to let it in,
To share my talent with everyone,
My journey had just begun
And now I'm sharing this talent
with the world,
The poetry inside me has been set
free
And now the words are leaving me
be when I need them to
Because I let them out through
paper and pen,
When I do it feels amazing,
So I share them online as well,
Letting out the hell that was once
inside,
It fills me with pride,
And I'm now so proud to say that I
am a poet
And a poet I will stay,
There's no way I will ever stop
sharing this talent of mine.

@petren33

 **z.b.sayed** ·

⋮

I Am

I am an empath
I feel their pain everywhere
But whenever in trouble
I see no one standing there.

I am an introvert
I love my solitude
My strength comes from within
I keep to myself, it's not attitude.

I am non judgmental
Whatever be the situation
But I am mocked every single time
For my own decisions.

I feel the pain when others cry
Their pain is mine, we are unified
I feel the power from within
I see thing's on the blind side.

It's not my fault that I can't fit in
Believe me I try
This is who I am, this is my story
Accept me for being I.

Z.B. Sayed

shawnlehto.lonewolfpoetry •
Harbor City Estates

I am whatever I need to be in the moment
To other's ways, I am not a proponent
Sometimes your friend, sometimes your opponent
And if I wrong you, give me my atonement
I can't bow down and not be myself
My truthfulness, to me, is my greatest wealth
I would love to live my life in stealth
Most people in the world affect my health
I am what no one else wants to envision
A hopeless being, who can't make a decision
On a crash course with Death, imminent collision
Between joy and pain, a wide division

shawnlehto.lonewolfpoetry •
Harbor City Estates

I am more than most can handle
But they are attracted to me, like a moth to candle
It's obscene, I dont want most to get too close
Most of my time, I spend being morose
Sure I can fake being excited for awhile
But when you leave, I eviscerate that smile
My internal fears run a country mile
In truth, my demons, I do revile
I wish to be different, but that fight I won't engross
If only it was easy enough to give me a dose
But wouldn't that create a worldwide scandal
If you were to take it all away, like a vandal

shawnlehto.lonewolfpoetry •
Harbor City Estates

I am my truth, but I live all your lies
Or is it seemingly, the other way around
I've heard the screaming and snuffed those cries
In hopes I can locate what you hoped I've found
The GPS system can't map out the directions
And leaves me lost, on my way back to my glory
The roads back dont have intersecting connections
So I'm stranded here, to finalize my own story
I am a wanderer, seeking to validate my reputation
In search of finding my unequivocal proof
Yet i am still stranded at the last wayward station
Of being all of my lies and living your truth

shawnlehto.lonewolfpoetry •
Harbor City Estates

I am full of my own hyperbole
I believe my constraints are what you don't see
You don't feel the things about which i ruminate
While inside of you, your soul is prostrate
You can't open that box and not suffer
Between yours and my demons, I am that buffer
I would love to live in a world so bucolic
But I am here, as a practicing alcoholic
So leave me here to escape, as I imbibe
To all your ways of living, I am unable to subscribe
I exist so that you can point out my various flaws
But in the end, it is I, that creates my own laws

shawnlehto.lonewolfpoetry •
Harbor City Estates

I am whatever it is that i need to
be *pectations*   *Reality*
I was born to obliterate my own
destiny
I'm not a mindless drone, defeat,
i do accept
In fact, it is the only thing, out of
myself i expect

storm_writing •

I am a fucking contradiction
perhaps a trauma cliche,
the cocktail of spirits that
you never should have mixed.
I am the charcoal clouds gathering,
storm that is approaching,
monsoon of violence floods the levels,
scarring the only ones I love.
Extreme emotions harnessed with haste -
the frightened one has cracked open
the inside of my head and
I am laid out across the sky,
spinning with uncertainty.
Every yes that was silently a no,
every secret I kept with his name in my mouth,
shame in my veins and a monster in my bed.
Little bird with broken wings,
the Ash Girl goth stuck in my dreams,
blood and ink combined on a page,
and twenty years rescuing a hungry ghost.
I was lost and pitiful for so long but now
I am learning to be free.

z.b.sayed •

                                                       ⋮

I am a girl child, I was born this way
I know I am not a son, don't take my life away
Education is my right, I can be someone someday
I don't belong in the kitchen, I am a kid who just wants
to play.

I am a girl, who is trying to understand this world
Opportunities for me are low
Marriage is what my parents are looking for
My looks are the only thing that matter
The better I look, the richer I marry, the higher will be
my stature.

I am a married woman, with a family of my own
In every decision I make
Permission is a must, as you know
Because my husband is my God
And my in-laws are my shadow

I am a mature woman, my old age has begun
First, my husband was my God
Now it's my son
My job is to bring home my son's bride
Inside the house she will be our slave
In society, she will be our family's pride.

From where I belong
This vicious cycle is an accepted norm
Society still conforms
From where I belong.

— Z.B. Sayed

YourQuote.in

jellybeantoespoetry ⋮

I am
a patchwork bag.
Cross stitches of hope and back stitches of yesterday
keep me together. Sometimes I carry
the weight of the world
and unravel.
Countless times I have fallen apart.
Countless times hope patches me up.
Yes, I have pieces,
maybe that's what makes me so strong,
protecting my delicate lining.
By the way,
don't pull those loose threads-
I am sensitive.
I hold everything inside.
I used to envy fancy bags.
I wanted to be noticed,
but now,
I prefer being priceless.
I am a patchwork bag
my fragmented remnants
make me whole.

@jellybeantoespoetry

rosa.g.words •
Lawley Village

I am...

I am a speaker of truths
a warrior of convoluted words
twisted and spoken left beside you,
a soothsayer
saying much that has soothed
and hushed the restless mind,
a dreamer of impossibilities,
the flightless bird adorned like the phoenix risen,
and ridden as the goddess of love and lust, the whore
and the saviour both.
I am the nightmare where dreams come to feed
and a world devoid of people.
I am loved and loathed, hunted but never found,
root bound yet free, scorched earth and dessert sea,
I am this and everything yet to be known.
I am all of this, a chaotic seed bruised wide open
spell cast and wind blown.
@rosa.g.words

samyukta_81d ⋅

I am a paper airplane
Built for games and smiles
Though given the right push
I could go for miles

The first flight's never perfect
Improvements will be made
So even when I hit the dust
I'll hope to fly again

I am a paper airplane
My wings are thin and frail
But the loving hands that made me
Will make sure I won't fail.

~Asta

 e.tstockdale_ •

I am a bleeding heart
Running out of time
Who once wanted to be somebody
But also wanted to hide

I plunged into the deep end
Before I knew how to swim
Before I knew
                    anything
Mistakes
        Mistakes
Held me down
Watched me as I drowned

In a pool of red
Arms stretched wide
Conversations with the sky
Are days gone by

What I would have done
        If I had more time
What would have happened
        If I didn't run and dive?

Just to be hidden
bleeding
    out of sight
In a pool of red
Arms stretched wide

-        etstockdale

poetry_in_moments_ •

I am...
A Poet

I am the body, made up of stars
i am the way, led up by scars,
of all the days, those bygone far,
pathway to past, the doors ajar.
spinning round my own small world,
no sun to shine but light to hold,
deja vus of times undone,
twisted thoughts regretting some,
no marks left off of tracking stones,
expressions few from flesh to bones,
through silence some, sometimes the touch,
sometimes unsaid no moments such,
made up of skies, the mostly dreams,
look up for chance whatever seems,
the unfelt feels, but head's a farce,
creating stories of different parts,
i am the lie, i am the write
i am the lines of what i might,
bleed off the inks, unsure the truths,
the made up lies untruly soothes,
i am the dark, i am the glam,
uncertainty, is what i am.

© Poetry in Moments

133

debbie_o_bottled_up_feelings ·

⋮

I am a poet
Because I create words
That create feelings
In myself and others
I am a poet
Because I take my craft
Very seriously
It is my life
These words bleed before me
And I give them to you all
I am a poet
Because I bare my soul to you
The public
To love or hate
I am a poet
Because I am driven
To write
I am a poet
And I shall die this way

debbie o bottled up feelings

 ellie.writes2 ·

I am a poet
My heart sings when I am happy
This pen grows wings
Words fly off the page
But my words burn when I'm enraged
My pen becomes a weapon
Words stabbing with each phrase
In sadness my heart aches
My pen bleeds the heartbreaks
Words flow like tears dripping from my
heart
Tearing the world apart
I am a poet,
This is my art
E.W.

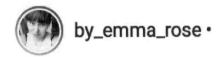 **by_emma_rose** •

⋮

*I AM a mother, first and foremost
I AM someone's daughter, someone's partner and
a friend to most
I AM doing my best to be the best that i can be
I AM working hard to show my kids and the world
the best of me
I AM not perfect and i have flaws too and i have
off days like like the rest of you
I AM here on a road less travelled, where God is
mighty and I trust in him
I AM one in a world of billions but feel my importance
given from him
I AM living
I AM here
I AM me
I AM*

namans_words ·

I am
the labyrinth
leading myself astray,
the protagonist
of my own play,
head over heels
for the ones with heart,
petrified when pierced
by their word-darts,
at ease and at peace
when surrounded by none,
an owl with a soul -
dark as night, with night at one,
an ocean of emotions
with no nerve of steel,
many things yet nothing
that you may call ideal.

naman

 ruji.writes •

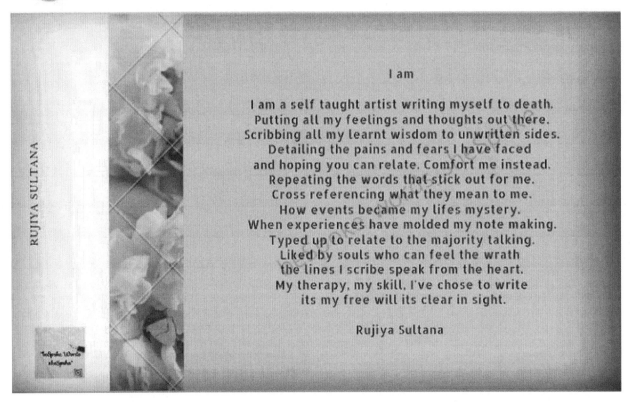

RUJIYA SULTANA

I am

I am a self taught artist writing myself to death.
Putting all my feelings and thoughts out there.
Scribbing all my learnt wisdom to unwritten sides.
Detailing the pains and fears I have faced
and hoping you can relate. Comfort me instead.
Repeating the words that stick out for me.
Cross referencing what they mean to me.
How events became my lifes mystery.
When experiences have molded my note making.
Typed up to relate to the majority talking.
Liked by souls who can feel the wrath
the lines I scribe speak from the heart.
My therapy, my skill, I've chose to write
its my free will its clear in sight.

Rujiya Sultana

z.b.sayed •

I am who I am
I will always be
I am myself
I don't need your approval to be me
Looks are not the only thing that you want to see in me
Let me introduce you to the power inside me, called she
If you ever get to meet my personality
I bet you will run for your life, I guarantee
I own my own destiny
I am my own reality
If looks are all you see in me
Too bad that's your failed ability
I'd love to be in love with you
Minus your insecurity
I'd love to be in love with you
If you give me the respect I give thee
If I were you, I would absolutely adore me, because
I am who I am
And I will always be
I am myself
And I don't need your approval to be me.

Your**Q**uote.in

— Z.B. Sayed

 gothrulz ·

Poet

I'm a poet

And with my quill the words do flow

Let the blood stream, cut me open

For this gift to me the universe did bestow

All that you feel will be spoken

For I can put on paper all that you are scared to show

Onto that parchment I can spill that emotion

Why the words come to me like water, I will never know

Make your heart swell, hit you like an explosion

From my fingers to that page the ink does glow

Make you feel like you have taken a potion

Into your soul my words become interwoven

In vain I hope I did not spill this hemoglobin

Come swim in the depths of my ocean

By Sara Brunner 2021

moderndayblake ·

I am... against society

I am steadfast when they tell me to flee,
I regress from calm because I feel at home at the
I am the ring on your finger,
When I should be the palm,
Steady in flow
No housewife so strong.
I am the pregnant belly
You chose to ignore,
Sweeping past
Unfathomable shores,
Waddling across classes -
Roller suitcase across the masses.
I am the golden sister,
Where jealousy stirred
Blood-soaked fists
My entire childhood a blur.
Chose to put distance
Between the only family I knew
To venture into charted territories
Of green and sky blue.
I am the wife
Who put her entire life
Into a love that no one else found.
I am the success story
Who got the family
And refused society's notion of bound.
I am the one who rejects the choice
Between family and career.
The daughter, friend and mother
To all those I hold dear.
Constantly exploring
The unknown glories
Set forth amongst a few.
I am a beacon when I'm told
No longer should I be bold.
Well fuck society -
I am one of a kind.

 **nikkomedeiros** •

Im A Panda

Im still dying, but only on the inside.
Still want to hide my face, but cant hide.
Im strapped in for the long ride.
Been roughed up, like I got raw hide.
My skins been bumped, bruised, and burnt.
Been cut, stabbed, discarded like dirt.
Dug deep, destabilized... No matter the hurt.
Im fixing my worth. Or at least my perception.
Step to the panda, get met with aggression.
Not about violence, its just for my protection.

secret_words_of_hart •

⋮

@SECRET_WORDS_OF_HART

I AM A WORD FINDER
A BRAIN WONDERER
SQUEEZING OUT WORDS
OTHERS UNHEARD
TO GIVE ME A VOICE
WHEN I HAD NO OTHER CHOICE
I COULDN'T SPEAK
WHILST THE POISON DID REEK

 d_b1226 ·

I am a poet

Because feelings

need to be written down

To understand what they bring

And to accept what they take

~ Daniela ~

nofilterneededforinspiration ·

The Midnight · Lost Boy

⋮

0:00 remaining

I am.....

I am a little bit weird,
Emotionally awkward once upon a time,
Like broken Lego,
I don't quite fit. or fall in line,
I am hard to understand,
Some say my humour is wild,
The villain of someones story,
I am forever exiled!
But this is me,
and can I ask,
who else can I be?

~justluke

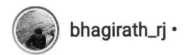 bhagirath_rj · ⋮

I want to believe,
I have grown up as a man.
No gender bias,
A human male specie, I am.
Away from 'my way or highway' attitude,
Self-titled free, in real, careless,
Almost borderline rude.
And you should have seen me brood.
Silliness, still unexplained, worn down.
Impatience, thankfully, gone down.
Trophied Remnants of past remain,
Shaping me, shading me as human.
A unique soul in seven billion.
Chasing dreams, yet to be seen.
Hiding leaky bandages,
Some gifted, some self inflicted ones.
Part time rebel, full time dreamer,
A kingdom, a prince and a queen.
Route seems long, uneven, quiet,
My pen says, I am right,
I believe, I am.

@bhagirath_rj

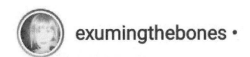

exumingthebones ·

I am unfinished in my perfected
darkness..in my hauntedness..
 In my hot mess..
I am but started to unfold my weaving
 of the deceiving and my disbelieving..
  this complicated complex..

And I, the word braider..truth trader
 for the secrets that dare crave home..
Will autopsy and dissect
  Trauma's Virus
  after I exhume these bones..

I AM COMING
 have no doubt..for I have
  just begun…
Hide your precious predators..
 Cuz I PROMISE..
  I AM COMING AT YOU
  'TILL YOU'RE DONE

  …

  KJF

  …

  kjf

 s.j.m.creative •

I AM
ITCHING, DISORDERED, ETCHED STATEMENTS
CARVED INTO PULPED WOOD,
THOUGHTLESS, RAMBLING LITANIES
CAST ASIDE IN THE MARGINS
OF A NOTEBOOK OF MADNESS.
DRIFTING, INKY CHARACTERS
SET OVERBOARD CARELESSLY
MEANING LITTLE TO NOTHING
INDIVIDUALLY, COLLECTIVELY.
I REQUIRE A SEAMSTRESS
TO PATCH ME TOGETHER,
YET IT SEEMS
THERE IS LITTLE MARKET
FOR THAT ARTISAN TRADE ANY MORE

Stuart Mckellar

inksanityyyyy ·

I am....
sorry
Ian....
let me start again,
I am ET
after
the OP
I'm a opet who can't smell
a poet who can't spell
like a useless witch....
She glued her broom
so it sticks
I hid my arms
in a pit
now my guns
stink like sweat
a little bit,
18 billion nipples
but 9 billion tits
1 billion brains
8 billion just exist
5 billion poets
on the same
waiting list
with tongues
that talk french
but have
never been
kissed,
writings about levels
like a 90s perm
but for some
it's 90s curtains
on the fringe
but never earn,
they'll never make the cut
so somethings always
in their eyes,
they question wisdom
"why's"
which isn't wise,

and they got front

which they can't back

but they still stand

by their lies.

Inksanityyyyy.

shawnlehto.lonewolfpoetry ·

Harbor City Estates

⋮

I am a shape that takes no form
I am the opposite of the social norm
Like hell's fire, I'm more than warm
I am the eye, in nature's storm
I am a slight modicum of your doubt
I am what your mother warned you about
Like a noise that makes no sound
I am a gravestone in the ground
I am a plague upon your land
I am worse when I'm out of hand
I am a nightmare that ends in a dream
I am a name, you refuse to scream

shawnlehto.lonewolfpoetry •
Harbor City Estates

Whatever i am, it's because of you, I'm here
I am the one to expunge your fear
I am solace when your life is astray
I am the rope you hold that never shall fray
I am a poet who knows no words
I am a song that's yet to be heard
I am the voice that beckons you to stay
I am the road when you run away
If you heed the warnings, I am a force
I am your protector, if you stay this course
Stick close here always by my side
I am no leader, but for you, I'll guide

shawnlehto.lonewolfpoetry •
Harbor City Estates

⋮

I am the words that make no sense
I am the biggest fraud, I am pretense
I'm your excuse, when the truth you can't face
I am your shelter when you just need space
I am a friend when your life's out of control
I am inside, but I'm not your soul
I am the thread to sew up your wounds
To your cries i am attuned
In your artistic ways, I am your muse
I am a decision you'd hate to choose
I am a recording of your innermost thoughts
But i am not the solution for validation you sought

shawnlehto.lonewolfpoetry ·

Harbor City Estates

What I'm not is what you seek

The answers to the question, the days of your week

I am not the one in which you can rely

I'm not the sunshine in your sky

I'm the one bound up in those chains

I'm not the genius in your brain

I'm only the dark thoughts, the world disdains

I'm not the one you should restrain

I am one you should decry

I'm not the one you should pass on by

I am tears that fall, whn your eyes leak

I am not to bold and yet I'm not meek

shawnlehto.lonewolfpoetry •
Harbor City Estates

I am the junction when your road splits in two
I am the thing you should always do
I am the reckoning at the end of your world
I am the chaos your lies have unfurled
I am the difference in the things you say
For I am you at the end of the day

 **lishid619 ·**

I know I'm a good cook

I've made quite a few dishes in this lifetime

But I'm not a perfect cook or a professional chef

And I really don't know a lot of the recipes you ask for

That's why I've rejected many of your invitations

To be part of your recipe books

I would really like to cook along with you all

But I sadly am not that capable chef

Many of you like my food, many don't

I know I follow a very orthodox style

I know my recipes are odd and complex

But I started cooking for my own liberation and I still do

Yet I do wish if more people had tasted them

Gave their feedbacks and compliment them

Inspire me further to cook, to keep cooking

To discover more styles and recipes

There are spices still unknown to me

There are ingredients forbidden in my caste

There are cuisines hated by family

And I cook to explore and explode them all

I know I'm a good cook

But not sure if I can be the best

I don't know if I'm trying to be the best

I don't know if I want to be the best

But I do enjoy cooking

Cooking these poems

Even though I don't serve to satisfy many

But at the least for my own sustenance

Lishid Mohamed

sticksandstonespoet •
Melbourne, Victoria, Australia

I am the blackest sheep
the outsider
the one who could
have had the world
I reject your world
of hate and segregation
my world is full
of love and liberation
your so called standards
the underdog
who fears no god

I can't hear and obey
your rules of living

@sticksandstonespoet
@dmccarthy

Quotes Creator

onceapterousbutterfly

I am the host,
to a parasite,
in my brain,
who tells me,
that I am worthless ,
I am nothing,
& there is no refrain;

until today,
the world seems,
different & the ghosts ,
in my throat , that haunt me,
spoke quietly of the shame,

I am no longer a little girl,
I am part woman, part phoenix,
& under the full moon I wax and wane;
learning lessons and shedding scales,

I now make fire out of pain
& walk freely through the flame

By Carolina Troy

 sharz_world •

I AM A POET
MY TEARS SHED AND PRINT WORDS ON PAPER
MY SOUL IS BARE LIKE A NAKED IMAGE DRAWN ON CANVAS
FOR ALL TO SEE THE BATTLE WITHIN ME WILL JUST BE MY
CREATIVITY
THE MOST HAPPIEST MOMENTS OF HISTORY ARE WOVEN CAREFULLY
TO A PERFECT PICTURE SCENE TO REFLECT ON
A SHROUD OF COLOURS MAGNIFY MY PERSONALITY IN THAT
MOMENT
FOR ALL TO SEE THE BATTLE WITHIN ME WILL JUST BE MY
CREATIVITY
THE OUTPOUR FLOODS RIVERS THAT FLOW DEEP INSIDE, AT TIMES A
CRIMSON COLOURED STREAM SEEPS FROM MY FINGERTIPS AND STAIN
THE PAD
BRINGING TO LIFE THE DARKEST LINES OF MY SOUL JUST...
FOR ALL TO SEE THE BATTLE WITHIN ME WILL JUST BE MY
CREATIVITY
WHEN MY HEART CONNECTS A MYSTERY UNFOLDS THE WONDER OF
WHAT WILL BE, WILL BE REVEALED, JUST KNOW ITS CONFUSED
EMOTIONS WORKING ITS WAY TO SENSE
LINES OF TRUTH, HOURS SPENT
FOR ALL TO SEE THE BATTLE WITHIN ME WILL JUST BE MY
CREATIVITY

SHARZ_WORLD

thediffidentspeaker ·

⋮

I am nothing but a fleeting moment
The hand of a clock running in full circle
I am of life and love and confusion
Sometimes, I am nothing but paper
Floating and then soaked in water
Until I am dissolved and indecipherable

I am an unfinished chapter, a story never written
I am a leaf floating and then falling
Touching dust as if that was the ending
I am who I am
A moment passing in time and eventually forgotten
I am nothing but the beginning of endings

I am a drop of ink and then a piece of paper
And then whatever it is that I can use
Just to define and point out that I am abstruse
I am a flower that blossoms and then withers
A subject of life that is already dead inside

I am who I am, said the philosopher
Then again, after a few years of existence
I ask myself, "Who am I?"
I've never been close to the answer
For I am defined by a series of words
Coming and going, until eventually
For countless of times, I'll just lose my meaning

@thediffidentspeaker

full_moon_poetry •
Nashville, Tennessee

⋮

I am resilient.
I am the burned forest floor.
I was on fire.
I became desolate.
There was nothing left that wasn't singed.

And from that fire
Released billowing smoke.
And in that smoke
I could see every side of me.
Especially the ones I didn't want to see.

And that fire raged.
My fire raged.
Every spit from the fire
Was my truth longing to be set free
And it was.

 **full_moon_poetry** ·
Nashville, Tennessee

I simmered for months.
I looked defeated,
But *I am resilient*.
And my soul is now rich from the ashes.
Fertile with healing.

I am giving birth to my true self.
I planted seeds of hope, seeds of fearlessness,
Seeds of strength, and seeds of love.
I am growing now.
My roots are stronger than before.

The foliage of my mind is healthy.
My synapses are firing.
I am resilient and this is my forest.
Sometimes we just have to burn it all down
So we can build it back up.

-Full Moon Poetry

michellejschoultz ·

"I am…"

I am feeling consumed by an array of emotions.
Possible diagnosis? Borderline Personality Disorder or perhaps
its Bipolar…
They are profoundly deep; like the abysses of the oceans.
Their vastness is incomprehensible – I have absolutely no composure!

I am convinced the causality is due to a collection of uncertainties.
All ambiguity is the fons et origo of my self-diagnosed Anxiety, Depression
and significantly more.
These overwhelming feelings of stress seem to endure a multitude of
eternities…
What do I do? The turmoil of my thoughts are in a constant state of war!

I am an emotional eater, undoubtedly on the dangerous verge of binging.
Occasionally this triggers purging. Is this the genesis of my possible Bulimia?
The one to "rule them all", the debilitating "ring" of over thinking.
Paralyzing fear and worry take hold; this could very well be Lypothymia!

I am physically exhausted. Mentally fatigued. Emotionally jaded. Spiritually
weary.
My yearning for an aeonian slumber is beguiling and preoccupies my mind…
Quiet introspection of my theories often leaves me instinctively eerie, dreary
and exceptionally teary.
I appear to have progressive symptoms of Clanging – my mindset has clearly
rapidly declined!

~ Michelle J. Schoultz

maria_at_40 •   ⋮

I am failing,
daily.
Bad moves,
missed steps,
false starts
and dead ends.
The end?
Not quite....
I am growing,
exponentially.
Bad moves
educate.
Missed steps
reinforce.
False starts
refocus.
Dead ends
enlighten.
I am living.

 emme.gram •

      ⋮

I am climbing in reverse,
from the peak to the shit,
my hands holding on still
to each piece of the wall.

But I'm not crumbling down,
it is not that kind of situation
when you lose your balance
and concentration at once,
there
    and
       then
         you
           get what gravity means,
           displace your hips with a hit
           on your ass and just wish
           that was your head, instead.

 emme.gram •   ⋮

I'm wide awake at every step.
My fingers have been powdered
to stick to the grips, to grab the holes
in the rock, the hopes in the stones

at every inch - yet they frantically slip
bleeding right from underneath the nails;
two red trickles on the upper lip escape
the nostrils and color up my face. Got my
eyes
    on
      the
        prize:
            my head is upside down though,
            the golden statue is on the floor
            and I fear so much the height,
            the thought of it'll make me fall.

emme.gram •

⋮

So I am choosing to crawl, to be
in control as I reach the bottom,
but that's never getting close, close
enough to let it go, to let me go

down the hill, whisk in a spiral
before spreading my wings and
land on my feet. I grit my teeth,
I resist, I persist, not gonna bend
down
    on
        my
            knees
                just because I can't fold them,
                maybe. I am not as strong as
                I sound as I wait to lie on the ground,
                I want to go nowhere, I can go anywhere

                              from there.

benjaminsart77

I AM...

I AM the metaphoric bringer of rain
I AM laugh now cry later in pain
In the days of awe
I began to draw
To sketch my rage out
Before I tore the page out
I AM color revolution
Representing solution
Merging my red summers
In winters so blue
So ready for my breakthrough to you
I am you and me collectively
Are you proud of me?
I AM the hero and villain of my own story
I AM the protagonist
Glory no glory
Both facing the monster within
A night times burgundy grin
From an inside joke held in sin
I AM the hurricane you can't constrain
I AM the shadow boxer who thrives off pain
In the forecast of thunder and purple rain
I AM the rain dance
Taking a chance for a chance
All in one glance
I AM nothing less than a calculated guess
Of what could come next...

@BenjaminsArt77

 c__critz ⋮

I am a living breathing
toxic vermin of leaching germs;
feed me your insecurities and negative tendencies.
so that I can live off your fear forever,
as you reincarnate again.

c-critz

 **itsbrittaneibby**

I am a woman with a sacred womb.
I can nurture and birth spiritual life.

I can nurture and birth spiritual life.
Hallowed dreams flew from the cage of my soul.

Prayers and dreams flew from the cage of my soul.
On the alter of the sky i am blessed.

My voice i lift to the sky i am blessed.
A royal robe of purple adorns my flesh.

His Bronzed steel body adorned my flesh.
Our love is royal and spiritual.

Divine love is royal and spiritual.
Vibrating and offering a gift of self.

Vibrating and offering a gift of self.
I can grow hope in my sacred womb

brittneyreanne_writes

⋮

I am self-doubt
and hatred wrapped
in the baggy sweater
you wear every day.
I am the tears
running down your cheeks
and I'm the meals you skip
so you can feel skinny.
I am the guilt
and hatred in the
picture you won't post
because you're "too fat".
I'm the crumbs you leave behind
when you overeat and I'm the
loneliness that triggered you
in the first place.
I am your eating disorder,
and I'm eating you alive.

-Brittneyreanne

riddlingshrift
Old Saybrook State Boat Launch

⋮

I am...

Gregory Corso, locked
In Corrigan,
Writing poetry
On cigarette wrappers—

Robert Frost, callous-handed,
Telling the critics
To eat themselves
With their green sneers—

The ghost of Sylvia Plath, Heaven-sent,
Pleading
To bullied, torn women,
"Me, too—"

Christina Rossetti, sun-kissed
In a sunken garden,
Whisp'ring
With pink petals—

Paul Dunbar, trapped by hate,
Navigating race
Through language
Conventions and wisdom—

RiddlingShrift, an enigma,
Translating diverse stories
Of words
For your pleasure—

A poet.

@RiddlingShrift

b_christie_1242

I am a cloud watching the
sun fade into your
everlasting smile
burning in the mouth of stars
shining from the moonlight
to your golden flecks
beating with love
and desire swimming
in waves washed up
on shores of dreams
living in the hearts
perched upon a quivering
flower gazing into the eyes of
a sweetened bumblebee
flying in the breeze so
warm with song
singing on a stage with hopefuls filling
their cheeks with joy
praying for heaven to heal
the brokenhearted
walking in the darkest
nights to dream with
lullabies rocking
the insomniacs to drift
off and wake with
eyes open to the
brutal cruelty
towards sentient
beings starving for
hunger To save them
from the taste of greed
in the hands of a
child we will see
a new world rise in
open sky's painted
with strokes of
colours from the
pallet of a poet that I am

mysticlovepoetry

⋮

I AM A POET

Feelings that flow within our veins,
Outshines on paper for display.
I am a poet, vocabulary dances on my stage, while words act out a play.
Moving the heart and mind with thoughts that one could imagine or find.

We ink what we feel,
Some of it may not be real
Love, emotions, fantasy or tragedy,
Woven in form of poetry.
It isn't easy loving a poet,
not in ways you may know;
but through words that are meant from the heart and the mind can follow.

MYSTIC LOVE

 written_anomaly

⋮

I am a poet.
Electric words spark their
resurrection from my pen.
I am a poet.
Bleeding ruby emotions onto
an encrypted canvas of
conjured calligraphy.
I am a poet.
Fire spit it's glare into the
bed of my tongue with a
rapturous burning hot
enough for sin to melt.
I am a poet.
palm exploding sun's in my
mind's eye hoping to create
a universe to live in.
I am a poet.
I live, I breathe, and I love
poetry.
i am a poet.
And I wouldn't have it any
other way.

-Anomalous

I am
a
Poet

 c__critz ⋮

I am not here
to over stretch
a moment,
that has been
lost to the past.
I am here to
create new moments
with myself and you
that will last.

c-critz

22.06.2021

wildernest_poetry
Washington D. C.

I Am a Poet
there are stories
which burn with an
internal passion
deep within the poet's soul
they do not rest,
they clamor...
tugging, pulling, ringing bells
toppling ink wells
like boisterous, incorrigible children
who must be heard
they are determined and relentless
to become...
the intense, endless fire
the poet's
internal passion

Wildernest

m.meanders •

I am conflicted
I am confused
I am a tiny bit amused
I am wondering
If you get it
Before
I am carried off the shore
I am distant
I am flawed
I am in total aw
Of the ocean
And it's vastness
I am nothing at all

@M.MEANDERS

 verorisingpoetry •

I am eclectic electricity born to
entice and enthrall through my
explosive expression.
Bound to this earthly vessel
of flesh and bones,
shattered heart still beating in pieces,
within.
A human temple
that can barely contain this wild soul
created from dreams, magic, pain,
and the wisdom of the ages.

— Vero Rising Poetry.

sling_lavender_ink
Turtle Island

I am

I am swimming towards the Moon
in the twilight of day
to sleep in a crater
damp and cold.

I am freezing off the marauding
expectations reflected,
single soul lifting from
the corner of your eye.

I am brandishing my tongue and pen
in a flurry of assault
to keep away
the monsters in the dark.

1/3

sling_lavender_ink
Turtle Island

As I toss and turn
damp, silken Moon ash,
I am camouflaged
from lacerations of circumstance.

Indemnify the cracks and holes
in my bones and single soul,
lye scathing surface wounds
soothing to unfettered fear.

I am swimming back to the Earth
through the dawn of eve
burning up through the layers
to get back to me.

sling_lavender_ink
Turtle Island

I am singing no broken tune
tending to my wounds
plaster, splints and gauze,
refine their use over time.

I am writing on a broken bone
that heard from the Moon
words are raw and lose their form
healing single stone souls.

As I take my tongue and pen
tardy from the swim back down
I am loosening their savour,
screaming into your face.

I am.

Marianne aka sling_lavender_ink   3/3

im_backagain6

I am a poet,
I may not always be pretty,
I may come Across heartless at times,
If you offend me,
That makes me write,
If you judge me,
I will inform you,
You are nothing to me,
Don't get me wrong I don't like everyone,
But I know where to draw the line
I will not comment and obviously not like
I will not follow you,
I will just step aside,
Live and let live is the motto,
As long as you aren't causing hate or harm,
I don't like everyone,
I don't expect people to like me,
But I'd like it if you'd just let me be,
If you don't,
Just know I will write all about you,
I will show your true colours,
So please if you don't like me,
Unfollow that's cool with me,
I don't need anyone's opinion,
I write for me.

broken.foxx

I am an enigma to my own self,
hiding in the shadows of midnight
only allowing the secrets shown in moonlight
to be my reality, the only truth on offer.
What was it you expected to find here?
I've done what I can to manipulate memories,
the few that didn't abandon me,
the few who cling to their origins of pain,
to be more than mere momentary
flickers of feeling across a face
I've never recognized less than each passing day.
There's a strength in the accountability being
held to only the self, not to anyone
else, who can't comprehend the sacrifices
to which I silently acquiesced, searching
for a peace, for a forgiveness,
for an acknowledgement, an understanding
no one can provide.
I try to travel light but my demons cling to their baggage,
to their beginnings born of a vengeful desire,
their possessions thriving in gains,
like a meadow of mushrooms multiplying
with each memory of a memory recalled in my mind,
seeking a forgiveness, an acceptance, an alliance
to mend the last of the fractures,
to grant a wholeness found in a bliss beyond
the physical pleasures I've hidden in to mask the misery
into a euphoria that can heal what's been beyond broken
for too long, finding freedom in an enveloping embrace.

poetsbtu1906 ·   ⋮

I Am

I am the broken pieces of a little girl
Washed ashore by generations of deceit
I am the words unspoken by families
Screaming no surrender; no defeat
I am the voices that were ignored
While fighting in the cold and bitter rain
I am the generations of Americans
Screaming for equality through change

I am the children of forgotten generations
Who chose to fight to survive this world
I am the broken promises of protection
Housed in every abused little boy and girl
I am change for future generations
That's still slowly drifting in the wind
I am the songs of freedom
That we weren't prepared to sing again

I am the laws handed down through generations
That's the beginning and ending of every fight
I am the impending knowledge we shared
But couldn't make the change overnight
I am the light left shining by our ancestors
To guide the next generations past violence
I am the words spoken by Dr. King, Malcolm X,
          And so many others
That's shown every generation... We refuse to be silent!!!

jaimeboey • Following   ⋮

The Run

I am the one, who has failed and grieved
Adversity brought poetry to me
Because my eyes open to see, ears to hear
I am a poet blessed with readers like you

When I run, I'm running for the life in me
The joy tasting fresh breeze, dried linens in the sun
Immersed in the smells, what is sweet, bitter or sour
I'm in seventh heaven with both feet grounded
As Mother Nature granted me a second chance

This is who I am, my story, it goes a long way
Snarl in the gentle eyes meet the eye of storm
Brought thunderous waves unto pebbled shore
Where home disguised the solid rock, I was torn

@jaimeboey

Slide 1/4

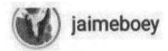 **jaimeboey**

The Run

Going anywhere, I carry gray cumulonimbus
That never pours, when I wake till my eyes close
Suicidal becomes an option for being a lost cause
Death in honour than to be marred dysfunctional

Torn ligaments, both knees and ankles
I could not carry with broken shoulder
Each move was like cracking eggshells
Creased lines had etched, grimace in pain
Disheveled when I reached my destination
My tears, my companion at night
My conscience during the day
To hide my grieve,
for honour and pride.

@jaimeboey

Slide 2/4

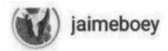

jaimeboey

The Run

Tell me how to live in the face of people
Who think I'm a disgrace in public?
Tell me how to savour the moments
When they look at me in horror?
Tell me what to believe when I'm alone fighting
For recovery takes time, is filled with sarcasm

I pause a while in reflection of courage
A quiet mind, transcends the peace comes from me
I've learnt to close my ears, be stilled my heart
Know that you cannot stop the scorn from others
But you can, to choose not to let it affect you
Break this stigma and be proudly beautiful

@jaimeboey

Slide 3/4

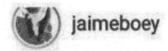

jaimeboey

The Run

I stopped running and sat on nearby bench
Overlooking the serene lake of memories
Weak winds rekindles flawsome scars
Who do I see in my reflection, who I really am?
I stand here not about my darkness
Or bask in glory *glitter in my wounds*
I will live on this tale to inspire you
So you will shine your inner light

You need not cry, there's an ocean
You need not frown, there are clouds
You're never alone, there's the moon and sun
You're never lost, stars constellate a path
You'll be alright, hear your Phoenix cry
Emerges from the ashes,

when it is you believing in you.
@jaimeboey

Slide 4/4

little_pearls_of_wisdom_ •

I am in short a miracle and Mohammad Hassan is my name
My difficulties are many but like you I am the same
I'm a gift from God to my devoted mother
I'm the eldest from my sister and brother
I'm autistic and I'm unique
Sometimes people find it hard to understand me as I speak
The benefits of being the way I am is I'm easy going and care for everyone
My true nature is be spontaneous and always be ready for fun
My mummy used to struggle with appointments and have sleepless nights
Because she said I had fits whilst sleeping which gave her the frights
Now she knows and understands as I get older
And she's proud to say I'm her little soldier
I have a habit of letting my mum know she's done something good
By kissing her hands as you know you should
And my mummy says it makes her feel like royalty
Mummy also says her heart melts at my loyalty
But for me I'm not special in any way
I just like routine everyday
In my happiness I hug everyone and tell them I love you
I must be special if you love me back too

c__critz

⋮

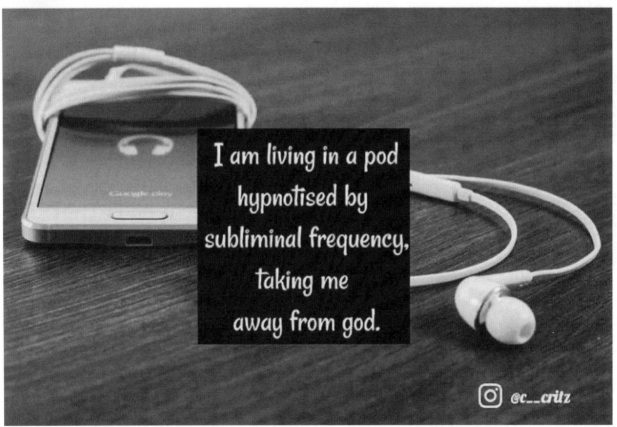

 s.j.m.creative •

I am closer now
Than I was yesterday.
There is still some way to go
Which doesn't matter anyway.
Step by step,
Day by day,
I am closer now
Than I have been any day.

Stuart Mckellar
@s.j.m.creative

ABOUT THE CURATOR

"Like some kind of semi-aquatic mammal, I've always felt I don't quite fit in, and I struggle to swim in certain streams for too long. I'm certainly not the most adaptable or flexible soul, and sometimes you'll spot me, clinging stubbornly to my clumsy armbands and hoping for the best. Try as I might, I'm always halfway in-between. But I do have a certain luminosity about me; my character dances from time to time, and ever occasionally, my personality shines through and sticks in people's minds. I have an aura of sorts and as a writer, artist and human, I hope that counts for something."

RDW

Ryan Daniel Warner, is a self-styled 'Writer, Artist and Human' hailing from Northern England - the 'Lake District' to be precise. He owns the Instagram account, @rdw.world, and the website www.rdw.world, which both showcase his various projects related heavily to poetry, writing and wordplay.

His debut work, 'Book One' – the first in an ongoing, life-long 100-part series is now available to purchase on Amazon and via his website. 'Book Two' is on its way (it's now way more than fashionably late). In addition, 'White Book' – the first in a series of 'Colours' will also be available "soon."

Ryan would also like you to know that he hates speaking in third person about himself, or pretending that somebody else has written the above, so he will end this anthology, characteristically, in first person by simply saying

Thank you to all involved.
To those who wrote such wonderful pieces,
and to those who had the pleasure of reading them.

PLEASE SHOW YOUR SUPPORT FOR THE AMAZING POETS INVOLVED BY FOLLOWING THEM ON INSTAGRAM AND CHECKING OUT THEIR WORK.

Printed in Great Britain
by Amazon

64512017R00111